# OF PRESIDENTS

# & PREDATORS

DAN BLACKBURN

PAGE PUBLISHING, INC.
New York, NY

First originally published by Page Publishing, Inc. 2018

ISBN 978-1-64214-511-3 (Paperback)
ISBN 978-1-64214-513-7 (Hardcover)
ISBN 978-1-64214-512-0 (Digital)

Printed in the United States of America

# FOREWORD

Old journalists' memoirs too often are mere reminiscences of big stories covered, places seen, and celebrities interviewed in the world of politics and entertainment. Dan Blackburn's retelling of more than half a century behind radio microphones and before cameras for scores of broadcasting stations and networks is all of that, but much more.

Beyond his close encounters ranging from Lyndon Johnson, Robert and Ted Kennedy, Ronald Reagan and Malcolm X to Sophia Loren, Ella Fitzgerald, Stan Kenton, June Christy and Linda Ronstadt, Blackburn's is a charming panorama of an earlier America, brought up to date.

It is told in the framework of his growing up in rural La Porte, Indiana, as the precocious but never pretentious son of a hard-working family who was smitten by the wonder of radio, music and eventually journalism, where he eventually found his niche.

His open and guileless manner brought him the friendship of the average joe and the powerful as well. In what perhaps was the centerpiece of his working career, on the campaign trail he became a favorite of Robert Kennedy. His accounting of the highlights from RFK's Senate career to the depths of his assassination in Los Angeles are among the memoir's most arresting.

Blackburn's breezy narrative often detours into other aspects of his journalistic life, such as his early love of music as a disc jockey and guitar-player in high school and college jazz ensembles that opened doors for him to so many world-renowned artists.

But in the end, it has been his solid grasp of the art of shoe-leather reporting, including winning the confidence of many of the great and no-so-great politicians and the respect of his colleagues that has marked his versatile career in one of the most demanding and competitive of communications disciplines, as seen in this informative and entertaining volume.

Jules Witcover, Syndicated Columnist

# Reflections on a Media Life

# CHAPTER 1

Life is a funny thing. It is about hopes and expectations. Dreams and disappointments. Sometimes you connect most of the dots. Sometimes all that's left are loose ends. And so it has been for me.

Harry Truman was the first president of the United States whose hand I shook. It was early autumn, in 1948, in northern Indiana. There was just a touch of a chill in the air when Truman's campaign train rolled into the station in my small town of La Porte. I was only 9 years old and my parents took me down to the station to see "Give 'Em Hell Harry" campaign from the train's caboose. As far as I know, he was the first and last sitting president to make a campaign stop there. It was only a few years later that passenger trains quit stopping in La Porte altogether.

Back then, train stations had an air of romance and mystery. People boarded trains to travel to faraway places like Chicago and Detroit and even New York. My brother Tom and I rode an old steam engine from time to time to visit relatives in central Indiana. Now, riding a train into our town, came this man about whom I knew very little but that he was president and came from Washington which was sort of like saying he came from China – a place far away. Later, I came to understand that he was running an uphill race for re-election against New York Governor Thomas Dewey. But, on that day, I only knew that he was somebody important who had come to my town and had shaken my hand. It would be twenty years later, in the spring of 1968, that another presidential candidate – Robert F. Kennedy – stopped in La Porte and I was traveling with him as a journalist assigned to his campaign and someone who was fairly close to him. In a sense, both were watershed events in my life.

I can't say that my parents were especially political. Nor were they apolitical. They voted for Truman and considered themselves Truman Democrats. After Truman, my mother tended to support Republicans and my father tended to say that he voted for the man and produced mixed results. However, they did talk about national and local events and discussed the news of the day at dinner. And they became a bit more involved when a friend and nearby neighbor – Harold Handley – was elected governor of Indiana. From time to time, he would drop by to visit and I often hung out within earshot and listened to the conversation. According to my mother, it was in that time period, more or less, that I first wrote and distributed a neighborhood newspaper. Fortunately, no copies of that youthful effort survived. But, during those early years, an interest in government, politics and world events grew within me. Maybe it was the end of World War II or Harry Truman's handshake or Harold Handley's visits or some combination of those and other things. But I soon realized that there was a wide and interesting world beyond the comfortable borders of the Hoosier state. And parts of that world would include some mighty four-legged predators.

As a youngster, I delivered newspapers – peddling my bike furiously over streets and down sidewalks to deliver the local bundle of news and advertising. I think I made about $1.25 per week. It wasn't bad during warm weather and I rather enjoyed it. But winter was another story. The wind would blow south from Lake Michigan and snow drifts often piled high and deep. When he could, my father would drive me along my paper route in his heated Oldsmobile. But often he would be away working, and I had to tough it out. One winter, when I probably was about 12 years old, my mother wrapped me in so many layers of clothing that I resembled the Michelin tire man. I finished my paper route and plodded toward home. At the bottom of the hill that led up to our street, I started feeling that I had to go to the bathroom. But the bathroom was many yards away and the temperature was well below zero. I struggled on and on and the need to go got worse and worse. Finally, I could not hold back any longer. A warm stream ran down my leg and froze right there. When I got home, my mother took the frozen clothes and hustled me off to a warm tub without saying a word. Winter in Indiana could be cruel.

Back then, television mostly was an abstraction. Other than newspapers, the main media that drew our attention was radio. I listened religiously to WGN broadcasting the Chicago Cubs baseball games, always hoping – then as now – for wins and stoically accepting the losses. We also listened to Arthur Godfrey's morning show, along with such kids programs as The Lone Ranger, Captain Midnight, The Green Hornet and more. Added to the mix were news broadcasts by Gabriel Heater, Edward R, Murrow, Morgan Beatty and the seemingly ageless Paul Harvey. When we visited my grandmother and aunts and uncles down on the family farm in central Indiana, we would huddle around an old and very large radio that held down a prominent place in the living room. My Uncle Bob would turn the dial and whatever was on the airwaves would fill the room with sound. It truly was a theater of the mind.

Eventually, of course, television edged its way into our existence. The flickering black and white images captivated us, although the first shows we saw usually featured professional wrestling with such stars as Gorgeous George. The news – short reports of no more than 15 minutes – was delivered mostly by radio veterans such as Murrow, Douglas Edwards and John Cameron Swayze. Rarely did our family miss those evening news reports. But the big breakthrough came in 1956, when the Huntley-Brinkley report was launched by NBC. "Good night, Chet. Good night, David" became a national catchphrase and, for this Midwestern teen, a symbol of what I wanted to do.

Our small high school was unusual in that it had remarkably high standards for its teachers. Many of them had Masters Degrees and the French, German and Spanish teachers were fluent in those languages. So, too, was the Latin teacher. We also had an aggressive drama class, a highly praised debate team, a prize-winning orchestra and marching band and a 15-to-20-piece dance band directed by Gene Pennington, a member of the late Glenn Miller's band.

My parents insisted early on that I take piano lessons and I did for at least 5 years, maybe more. I became proficient in reading as well as playing music. Then we also tried violin which quickly became a non-starter. Finally, my parents acquiesced to my repeated requests to let me take guitar lessons which I did for several years and continued to do off on over many years. All of this lead to my joining the dance band under Gene Pennington's direction.

**Blackie & Helen Blackburn**

As the lead guitar player in the band, I absorbed a lot from the director who had us playing note for note arrangements from his Glenn Miller days as well as music from such greats as Stan Kenton, Harry James, Benny Goodman, Duke Ellington and others.

I also was a member of a five-piece combo that was influenced by the jazz players of the day, especially Miles Davis, Chet Baker and Gerry Mulligan. In fact, our trumpet player – a very talented guy – was approached by bandleader Buddy Morrow to join his touring band. If you graduated from La Porte High School with good grades, admission into college was pretty much a foregone conclusion.

But the class that really caught my fancy was radio broadcasting.

We had a local radio station – WLOI – that played music, provided farm and weather reports, local news and a potpourri of programming. The radio station had offices over the local bank and one sunny day I brashly climbed the stairs and asked to see the manager. Sara Jane Keel, a fellow student in the radio broadcasting class, and I had an idea. We wanted to do a weekly radio program which we called "Those Teenagers". We would play records that were current hits and chat about what our fellow teens were doing. Much to our delight and surprise, the manager said he would make 15 minutes of air time available to us every Saturday. We had to fill it. And we did. A couple of months later, the manager came to us and said he had been hearing good comments and was expanding the show to a full half hour and we would have a sponsor. Eventually, the show stretched to a full hour with more sponsors and we even did live dance parties from the YMCA. We may not have been American Bandstand but, located just an hour from Chicago, we did get some attention and occasionally a rock and roll performer would drop by on his way to the Windy City and talk with us.

By this time, the radio station had become a part time job for me. They actually paid me to come in and do station breaks, read the news, deliver occasional sideline reports during high school basketball games – a very big deal in Indiana – and voice some of the commercials. I was just 16 when we launched "Those Teenagers" and I worked at WLOI until I went off to college. It was while working at the station that I covered my first real news story. A store in the downtown area had caught fire. I grabbed a tape recorder and rushed to the scene, describing the flames shooting up through the roof and the battle against those flames by the intrepid fire fighters. The fire chief even gave me an interview. By the time the fire was out, I was covered in soot, reeked of smoke and ash and was hooked on becoming a reporter. Look out Chet and David. I was coming down the road.

In fact, I brashly wrote a letter to the Chicago Bureau Chief of NBC News asking about the possibility of getting a job there. WMAQ was the NBC radio station in Chicago and it was my favorite station. I absolutely loved their hourly newscasts and vowed that someday I would work for NBC News. The Chicago bureau chief actually wrote back to me – a two-page letter that made a tremendous impression on a young wannabe reporter. He thanked me for writing to him and explained that NBC News had a policy of only hiring reporters with wire service or similar experience. He said that being able to write on a tight deadline was very important and that I should consider first working for the Associated Press or United Press wire services and added that a college education might be a good idea, too. He closed by saying that he was impressed by my letter and that he would keep it on file and that I should keep him informed of my progress. Wow! Years later, when I was a bureau chief, I hope I paid him back a bit by making sure that I responded to each and every letter of hope and application that I received. And that is how I came to hire Connie Chung. But that is a story for later.

# CHAPTER 2

In some ways, growing up in Indiana was a rather insular experience. The state is squeezed from the sides by Illinois and Ohio, partially cut off at the top by Lake Michigan and bordered on the south by Kentucky. World War II was pretty much an echo to us, although I do remember my father wearing an air raid warden hat and making the rounds of our largely rural neighborhood and all the church bells ringing on VE Day. Of course, we did listen to FDR on the radio with his fireside chats.

My father, A.D. "Blackie" Blackburn attended Purdue University, as did other members of his farming family, and began a career in highway and bridge construction working for a mid-sized company – J.C. O'Connor and Sons – that did construction work in Indiana, Michigan, Illinois and Ohio. That's how he met my mother, Helen, who was a young teacher in Illinois. In college, she'd actually met a dashing young student at a nearby school by the name of Ronald "Dutch" Reagan. They did not meet again until I reintroduced them during Reagan's 1980 presidential campaign. My parents moved to Xenia, Ohio, where my father was working on another construction job and where I was born. Shortly thereafter, they moved back to Indiana and, not long after that move, my brother Tom joined the family. For a time, we lived in a small house on the north side of La Porte, then moving to another rented house on the south edge of town outside the city limits. Eventually, my father built the red brick home nearby in which Tom and I mostly grew up. And he wound up establishing his own construction company – La Porte Construction – later run by my brother. However, money was in short supply while we were growing up. If we got a wagon for Christmas, my father built it. One Christmas, he built a two-story red and yellow barn and a green barnyard filled with animals for Tom and I. We spent hours with it.

My brother Tom and I had horses, helped grow our own fruits and vegetables – mostly by watering plants and pulling weeds – and rode bicycles, did chores, worked at whatever jobs we could find to make spending money and played basketball and football. Tom was an outstanding basketball player and went to college on a basketball scholarship. In the land of Hoosier Hysteria, that was a big deal. I really enjoyed the horses, eventually even doing some stunt riding and taking part in barrel races at the county fair and rodeo. Sometimes I just would toss a saddle on the horse, take some water and ride across the fields to a small pond where I would sit and watch the clouds float across the blue sky. A neighbor had a large piece of land nearby where he kept his horses and, in exchange for helping care for his animals, we could pasture our horse or horses there, too. In junior high, there were some days that I rode a horse to the little red school house (really) in the village of Door Village. They had hitching posts in front. An Indian battle was fought near there and a stone monument marks the spot. Ironically, my first girlfriend just happened to be a full-blooded Blackfoot and lived not far from where the battle marker still sits. Sometimes, we would ride double on my horse.

La Porte High School was a very different experience. Larger than any school I had attended before, it was blessed with some wealthy supporters. La Porte, itself, had a good tax base. In fact, it was remarkable for a small town and benefited from being relatively close to Chicago. Among the people who had homes there were the Singer family of sewing machine fame, Admiral Hyman Rickover, the dentist who invented the tooth positioner that children everywhere used, the man who invented the oil filter for automobiles, a family that owned woolen mills and a few others. As a result, the high school teachers were paid well and set strict standards.

One thread that ran through our lives during those years was the visits to the Blackburn family farm in Parker, Indiana. Parker was a small town in central Indiana where the train would stop from time to time. Riding the train there from La Porte was like stepping into a time machine. When you left La Porte, you travelled back to the early 1900's riding in the coach of a smoke and steam belching train or, less adventurously, in the back seat of my father's Oldsmobile. When we traveled by train, one of our aunts or uncles would meet us at the station. When we traveled by car, we usually headed straight for the old farm house and sleeping arrangements were decided there. Arrangements were necessary because the Blackburn family was large. My father was one of eleven children, two of whom died young. When aunts, uncles, in-laws, cousins and others were added to the mix, the family reunion became an event that each year was worthy of prominent mention in the local newspaper.

My grandmother was the family matriarch. She did not believe in modern conveniences. At the family farm, cooking was done over oil or wood fueled stoves. In winter, we had foot warmers with hot coals inside our beds at night because heat was mostly not available. Nor were bathrooms. There were chamber pots in the bedrooms. Otherwise, there was the outhouse. The youngsters were required to perform chores. For the younger ones, it was collecting eggs from the hen house. Others, depending on age, milked the cows, herded the cattle to and from the pasture, either on foot or horseback and slopped the pigs. The latter was considered dangerous because pigs are mean and, if you slipped and fell in the pig pen, it literally could be the end of you.

In the summer months, we also collected lightning bugs, played croquet and badminton on the front lawn, had picnics and rode the horse and buggy into town to watch the weekly movie that was shown on a screen hung in the town square. If we were big enough, we also rode the wooden drag behind the plow horses in the fields to break up large chunks of dirt into smaller chunks after the plow had gone through. Among the things my grandmother viewed with suspicion were dancing, playing cards and automobiles. One night, riding in the horse and buggy with one of my uncles, we saw strange lights in the sky ahead of us. They glowed and seemed to move under their own power. It may have been "swamp gas" but, for the longest time, I was convinced that space aliens were visiting rural Indiana. And this was long before the arrival of ET.

Every year, most of the cousins would climb on the back of the biggest plow horse for a group picture. We would squeeze tightly together from neck to rear. Two years in a row, my cousin Lucy fell off the rear of the horse and broke her arm. One other constant was the piano. All of the aunts were musically gifted and played the piano reasonably well. We would gather in the parlor where the upright piano rested and one of the aunts, most often my Aunt Pearl who lived to be over 100, would sit on the piano stool and play a wide range of songs with all of us trying, either well or badly, to sing along. I seem to remember that a big favorite was "Don't Fence Me In". If any of the grandchildren played the piano – and many of us did, more or less, a command performance was required. Today, much of this must seem terribly old-fashioned. But we all had a wonderful time and treasure those memories to this very day.

It was during this time that my interest in chemistry grew. I had an ever-expanding chemistry set which was set up in the back bedroom that I shared with my brother. There, I carefully did one experiment after another and became more and more confident. Eventually, I became intrigued with explosives and fireworks. In those days, you actually could buy many of the chemicals needed for explosives and fireworks at the local pharmacy. If they did not have what you wanted, you could order the chemicals from a supply store in Chicago.

In truth, then, as now, making explosives and fireworks required some experience and skill but still was relatively simple. At one point, I made nitrocellulose – better known as gun cotton – in a bathroom sink. Gun cotton, along with ammonium nitrate, was a principle explosive in canon shells used during the Korean War. I would hang the prepared explosive cotton up in the family laundry room so that it could dry very thoroughly. My mother knew it was some sort of a chemistry experiment, but I was careful to be vague on the details. Actually, gun cotton, by itself, poses little danger. If you light it with a match it just burns rapidly. However, if you compress it and use a fulminate or some other igniter, the result can be pretty dramatic.

Usually, I packed the cotton into used $CO_2$ tubes that served as propellants for model cars and planes or into empty shotgun shells. Then, I would attach a fuse made from string and potassium nitrate or some other source to light the tightly packed gun cotton. Once the fuse was lit, I would race away and then turn to watch the device explode in a neighbor's garbage can, sending the can soaring into the air.

I also made fireworks rockets and a launcher for the period around the 4th of July and would send the rockets into the night sky where they erupted in a variety of colors depending on which chemicals had been used to make them. Even my parents thought that was pretty cool. One day, however, I went too far. Working very carefully in my bedroom laboratory, I managed to produce the highly sensitive explosive nitroglycerine. This powerful explosive was the key ingredient that, when mixed with sawdust or other absorbent materials, was used in dynamite. I had about six ounces of the volatile stuff in a glass jar. The problem was how to dispose of it. My solution was to dig a hole in the backyard, put the filled bottle in the hole and replace the dirt so that only the top of the bottle stuck up above the ground. Then, I took a .22 rifle, lay down on the ground a good distance from the bottle full of nitroglycerine and fired one round into the exposed top of the bottle. The explosive result was loud and powerful. Big chunks of earth erupted from the hole. And my mother came running to see what had happened. With her hands planted on her hips while she surveyed the scene, she turned to me and declared, "Just you wait until your father gets home." Needless to say, he was not amused and I was grounded for quite a while.

Another type of power – this one a natural occurrence – also became familiar to us. Tornadoes would swirl through Indiana every spring and early summer. My father had built an underground shelter where we could hide should a tornado approach. Fortunately, we used it only once or twice. More often, we would marvel at the sheer power of the storm after it had passed. Pieces of straw would be driven into trees or through wooden planks. Cars and farm machinery would be tossed around like children's toys. You can feel the savage storm coming. The air seems to fill up with electricity, as the clouds swirl around in a funnel shape. Then, everything becomes very still. And very quiet. The leaves don't move on the trees and the birds fall silent. Suddenly, the roar begins and you duck for cover. Growing up, everyone learned to head for a ditch if you were in a car and saw a twister coming. One day, I was driving down a back road when I saw a tornado coming straight at me. I slammed on the brakes, jumped out and dove into the ditch. The tornado passed over me and missed the car and kept going, leaving downed trees and other damage in its wake.

During my high school years, I also worked for the Bernacchi family. Pappa Bernacchi and his wife were from the old country – Italy. Their sons were Joe, Harold and Bart. All three sons served in the Navy and won service wide boxing championships. Bart also became a fighter pilot. Joe took it upon himself to teach some of us how to box. Some of us became pretty good. The Bernacchis owned farm land just over the state line in Michigan. And they also had a large set of hot houses for growing flowers and other plants such as strawberries. Initially, I went to work in the fields where I weeded and sowed and performed all sort of chores, mostly on my knees with the cuffs of my jeans held tightly together with strong rubber bands. This was to keep out the dirt which included ash and literally could cut your knees very severely. Most of the people I worked with were men from Puerto Rico and, during one summer, I discovered that the ditches near the field featured natural growing marijuana. Eventually, the authorities made the same discovery and launched a campaign to exterminate it. We all rode to the fields in the back of a truck and returned home the same way. The Bernacchis provided lunch and, on the way home, snacks and bottles of homemade wine. Overall, it was good experience that really paid off one day when farm workers leader Cesar Chavez launched into a diatribe against the "Anglo" reporters at a news conference – reporters who he declared never had spent a day of their lives working in the fields. I knew Chavez and after the news conference I marched up to him and told him quite angrily that he was wrong and that I had worked for many hours on my knees in the hot sun. He apologized rather profusely, and we remained more or less friends. To this day, his partner in forming the

Farmworkers Union – Dolores Huerta – and I have remained good friends.

I always had been a card player. Canasta. Gin Rummy. Bridge. Whatever. My grandmother was an awesome card player. As I got older, she taught me how to deal seconds and thirds and read other players eyes. Imagine this 80-something woman teaching me not only how to spot cheaters but how to do it myself. I can easily say that my record in the Nevada gaming tables of never leaving as a loser is totally due to her.

# CHAPTER 3

In 1957, I graduated from high school. The Four Freshmen – all native Hoosiers at the time – were singing "Graduation Day" and diplomas were being passed out to the graduating seniors. Our band provided the music for the senior prom and I also interviewed attendees for the benefit of WLOI Radio. Most of us headed for the southern shores of Lake Michigan for a final round of very casual celebration that really was a toned down version of the many "beach" movies of the Fifties and early Sixties. Yes. Most of the guys really did wear their hair really short and poodle skirts and saddle shoes were part of most girls' wardrobes. The Crew Cuts sang "Standing on the Corner" and all of the guys did watch all of the girls go by. Vietnam had yet to become a factor. Dwight Eisenhower was president. Highways were being built. The cold war was the big foreign story, but we already had stopped ducking under our desks in rehearsal for an atomic attack. For many of us, the next step was college.

For me, there was little doubt about where to go for an advanced education. For a while, I considered the University of Michigan because I was attracted to their excellent chemistry department. But, since my family had a history of attending Purdue University, an outstanding science, engineering and agriculture school in central Indiana, tradition prevailed and off I went to become a Boilermaker. Of course, we had been attending football games at Purdue for years and the campus already was a familiar place. I joined another band and signed up for the judo team on which I competed through college. Much to my delight, the residence hall in which I lived had its own small but active radio station and I quickly won a slot as a residence hall station disc jockey. Purdue also has a superb university operated radio station – WBAA. The manager at the time was Johnny DeCamp – a cheerful man who also was the voice of the Purdue football games. WBAA played music but also had a polished radio theater program in which students delivered a variety of plays and other programs. I absolutely loved acting in some of the programs. My favorite was playing the part of gloomy old Eeyore the Donkey in a version of Winnie the Pooh. I also appeared on stage in several university theater productions including Cat on a Hot Tin Roof in which I received surprisingly glowing reviews. My senior year, the visiting artist was Shakespearean actor John Carradine – father of a generation or two of actors. I saw him the day he arrived on campus. He was walking up the steps to the arts building and wearing a fedora on his head, a cape swirled behind him and his black cane added more flair than support. I was awestruck.

At the same time, I needed to make some money. There were bills to pay. I had gotten married and my daughter Laura had been born. WBAA helped out by making me the first student ever to be paid for being on the air at the station. I also landed a job as an announcer and disc jockey at WAZY – the local commercial radio station. Both gave me some freedom to select my own play list of songs and, as a result, I was able to slip in the occasional big band track. In high school, I had become enamored with jazz and, especially, big band jazz. So, I would tuck music by Duke Ellington, Count Basie, Ella Fitzgerald, Sarah Vaughn, Benny Goodman, The Four Freshmen, June Christy and, of course, Stan Kenton into my programs. Stan Kenton was my hero. I had played the guitar and/ or bass parts for many of his songs while in high school and owned many of his albums. The Four Freshmen and June Christy were Kenton alumni and, during my four years at Purdue, I often had a chance to spend time with the Freshmen because they played quite a few dates in Indiana and the group's members were from my part of Indiana. I also got to hang out with Stan Kenton during those years and for some years thereafter. At one point, the Kenton band, including June Christy and the Freshmen recorded their acclaimed "Road Show" album during a concert in Purdue's widely recognized music hall. I was back stage for part of it and was asked by Stan to escort the charming Miss Christy around campus during band rehearsals. In addition, I was to make sure she did not stray to any place that sold alcohol. I even got to sit in with the band because I knew the charts and Stan, who was known for his encouragement of young musicians, sat down one evening and taught me to play "Intermission Riff" – one of his signature songs – on the piano. I was thrilled. Meanwhile, I continued to play with various small bands for events in and around the Purdue campus, as well as in the Chicago area.

Some ten years later, after I had moved to Washington, D.C., and was covering Capitol Hill, Stan appeared to testify before a Senate committee looking into the issue of music copyrights. He was accompanied by the drop dead gorgeous and sexy singer Julie London whose sultry version of "Cry Me A River" was a huge hit. During her testimony, Julie brought down the house by performing the Mickey Mouse song a cappella in her own unmistakably sultry style. You've never really heard the Mickey Mouse song until you've heard Julie London's version. No one ever spelled out Mickey's name letter by letter – M…I…C…K…E…Y – with such effect. To say that the senators were entranced would be an understatement.

Of course, college was not all fun and games. Purdue is a tough school and I was serious about chemistry. I also was lucky. Professor Herbert Brown – a Nobel Laureate – singled me out to be the only undergraduate to work in his lab on campus. At the time, he was developing a new propellant for the NASA space program. At one point, he handed me a beaker containing a mostly clear liquid and asked me to put it in the lab refrigerator. Out of curiosity, I asked what would happen if I dropped it. He replied, "Then where we are standing would suddenly become a very large hole in the ground." Because of my lab access, some of my friends asked me to acquire some very high proof lab alcohol for a fall party. I managed to collect about a quart which was dumped into a punch bowl to which fruit juice and other mixers were added. Unbeknown to me, the grad students were well aware of the temptation presented by lab alcohol and the amount that was left sitting out was deliberately mixed with phenolphthalein which has powerful laxative effects. Before long, a lot of people were running for the bushes, bathrooms or where ever they could find. The party came to an early and ignominious end.

Graduating from college brought with it the need to find another job. Although I had entered college planning to be a research chemist, I graduated with hopes of becoming a broadcast journalist. My summer experience of selling Kirby vacuum cleaners did not seem to be a line of work for me after graduation. So, I enthusiastically accepted an offer from WOC-TV and Radio in Davenport, Iowa, to join its staff. I was to be an announcer, disc jockey and news reader. We moved into a basement apartment on the north side of town where the snow covered the windows. WOC had quite a history in terms of radio broadcasting. At one time, it was the end of the line (or start of the line, depending on your point of view) for broadcasts to and from the East Coast. Bob Hope, Jack Benny and others actually had done their shows from the WOC studios not far from the banks of the Mississippi River. The station was owned by the Palmer family which had advanced the practice of chiropractic medicine in the United States. In fact, the station call letters – WOC – stood for "World Of Chiropractic". Students from their nearby school occasionally came by to give WOC staff members chiropractic adjustments to relieve the tensions of the day.

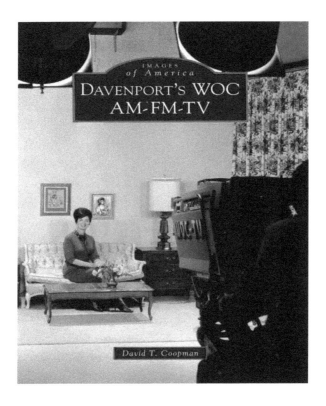

David T. Coopman

One of my jobs at WOC was to be the booth announcer who introduced the very highly rated 10:00 o'clock evening news. That news broadcast dominated the Quad Cities market and almost everyone watched it. As a result, it had a national sponsor – the Joseph Schlitz Brewing Company. My lines were simple. Every evening, Monday through Friday, I would say, "And now the ten o'clock news, brought to you by the Joseph Schlitz Brewing Company, Milwaukee and other cities." Then, the anchor, on camera, would say "Good evening" and the broadcast would be underway. In those days, fellow staff members occasionally would play pranks on their colleagues, trying to disrupt their script reading or ad-libbing. Once, one of them set my script on fire. Another time, they hired a local stripper to perform in front of me. I nonchalantly sailed right along without a break. Then, one night I tripped myself up.

It was on the introduction to the Ten O'clock News. I had done the introduction so often that I never even looked at the script. But, on this fateful night, I was inexplicably tongue tied. And the intro-duction came out as, "And now, the ten o'clock news, brought to you by the Joseph Shitz Bluing Company". The director, who I could hear in my earpiece, started to giggle. Then, the anchor began to chuckle and the cameraman was outright laughing so that viewers at home saw their video bouncing up and down as the camera shook from its operator's laughter. By then, the anchor could not continue and took an early break, throwing it to an announcer to do what then was a live commercial for Schlitz. It must have been the longest commercial of his life and he never really got all the way through it. The studio was in a state of hysterical laughter. The fifteen-minute newscast never really got off the ground that night and the next day several of us were fired. The station manager saw no humor whatso-ever in the incident.

Fortunately, another station in the market had an opening and I was hired immediately but remained there only briefly before being brought back to Indiana to work at WTRC Radio (an NBC affiliate) and WSJV-TV as a news reporter and anchor.

Based in the populous and economically important media market that included South Bend, Mishawaka and Elkhart in north central Indiana, the audience spanned Notre Dame University, the headquarters of the Studebaker car company, Conn-Selmer musical instruments, several key recreational vehicle manufacturers and the pharmaceutical company Miles Laboratories which later was taken over by the Bayer conglomerate.

It was here that my journalistic foundation really took shape. Our newsroom often partnered with reporters at the local newspa-per – the Elkhart Truth. This was especially helpful when trying to cover the police beat or city hall. For a time, I was the early morning reporter which, in the cold winters of northern Indiana, could be a challenge. More than once, the police department sent a squad car by my house to help jump start my car so that I could get to work on a winter morning. Sometimes, the officers even gave me a ride to work.

# CHAPTER 4

The relationship between reporters and police often is an interesting dynamic. I have worked with and around local police, sheriff's departments, state police and various federal agencies, including the Secret Service. Often, these officers can be suspicious, minimally helpful and, sometimes, hostile. Frequently, the job of an officer, deputy or agent and that of a reporter includes an inherent conflict. We want information that they may not want to share and, sometimes, we get in the way. Over the years, I developed working relationships and even genuine friendships with many officers and agents. I got to know, like and respect most of these outstanding men and women. I also met some genuine jerks, but they were very much in the minority.

Secret Service agents are a special breed. Their job protecting elected officials and dignitaries is difficult, demanding and, sometimes, dangerous. They are smart, dedicated, hardworking and often genuinely funny. Having covered a lot of presidential campaigns over the years, as well as the White House and Capitol Hill, I have spent quite a bit of time around the extraordinary men and women of the Secret Service and I have an abiding affection for them.

There are many Secret Service anecdotes. After Reagan was elected, the Secret Service placed agents on the perimeter of his ranch north of Santa Barbara when the then president was staying there. One summer afternoon, an agent on the perimeter dozed off only to be awakened when he heard a noise. He opened his eyes and found himself staring into the eyes of a mountain lion. Fortunately, both escaped unharmed.

Of course, there are female Secret Service agents, too. Often, but not always, they seem to take a somewhat more serious approach in their interactions with the accompanying press corps. One evening, I had asked one of the female agents to join me for a drink and a movie. The time for her arrival came and went and I began to wonder whether some emergency had occurred. Then, she arrived and explained that a supervisor had sprung a surprise inspection and, when she pulled her pistol out of her purse, there was a large wad of chewing gum stuck on the gun sight. The supervisor was not amused but we both got a good laugh out of it.

# CHAPTER 5

Meanwhile, time traveling back to Indiana, WTRC & WSJV were NBC News affiliates. On the radio side, they carried network newscasts featuring Morgan Beatty with his Paul Harvey-esq delivery, David Brinkley and Robert McCormick among others. The station also fueled my interest in politics as I got to know the then-national Democratic Party Chairman who also was a local attorney. At the same time, I developed solid relationships with Indiana Third District Congressman John Brademas – one of the genuinely smart guys – and Sen. Birch Bayh. The charismatic Bayh defeated incumbent Homer Capehart who simply had no idea of the impact of television on political campaigns and may have run the worst commercials I ever have seen. Bayh, who survived the small plane crash that seriously injured his friend Senator Ted Kennedy, was chairman of the Senate subcommittee on Constitutional Amendments and the principal architect of two constitutional amendments:

- The 25th Amendment, which established the rules for presidential succession and disability.
- The 26th Amendment which lowered the minimum voting age to 18.

And he was the leading Senate sponsor of the Equal Rights Amendment. He also was a leading candidate for the Democratic nomination for president in 1976 but dropped out of the race after his wife, Marvella, was diagnosed with cancer. Later, Bayh lost his

OF PRESIDENTS & PREDATORS

Senate seat to Dan Quayle who went on to become vice president under George H.W. Bush.

Then, one day, I received a phone call from the news director at WOWO Radio in Ft. Wayne. WOWO was then and remains a huge radio station with a clear channel and 50,000 watts of power. That means that the station shares its frequency with no one and we used to say of WOWO that it put all 50,000 watts out of the very top of its antenna. Its reach is so great that I even got fan mail from sailors at sea off the coast of Japan. One day of each week I worked as a disc jockey, again with the freedom to insert my own song choices into the playlist. The rest of the time, I was on the highly regarded news team. WOWO was part of the Westinghouse chain of radio stations and Westinghouse maintained its own news bureau in Washington, D.C., just like the bigger networks. Because the Westinghouse stations packed a lot of punch on the airwaves, they got a lot of attention and they took their news coverage very seriously.

In August of 1963, a group of civil rights leaders organized what became a very famous and successful March for Jobs and Freedom that culminated in front of the Lincoln Memorial in the nation's capital. I was assigned to travel with one of the buses making the trip from Indianapolis to Washington. There was a sense among all of us on the bus that this would be a very important event when all the marchers arrived at their destination. However, I do not think we realized how eventful it would become. President John F. Kennedy had initially opposed the march because he feared it could jeopardize his civil rights bill pending in Congress. More than a quarter of a million marchers filled all the sun-drenched space in front of the Lincoln Memorial and spread down both sides of the reflecting pool on the national mall. It was the largest protest gathering ever to that date in Washington.

For a young reporter from Indiana who had visited Washington just once previously as a child, it was an awe-inspiring event. Reporting on it live was a privilege as much as an assignment. And then the Rev. Martin Luther King Junior spoke.

*But there is something that I must say to my people who stand on the warm threshold which leads into the palace of justice. In the process of gaining our rightful place we must not be guilty of wrongful deeds. Let us not seek to satisfy our thirst for freedom by drinking from the cup of bitterness and hatred.*

*We must forever conduct our struggle on the high plane of dignity and discipline. We must not allow our creative protest to degenerate into physical violence. Again and again we must rise to the majestic heights of meeting physical force with soul force. The marvelous new militancy which has engulfed the Negro community must not lead us to distrust of all white people, for many of our white brothers, as evidenced by their presence here today, have come to realize that their destiny is tied up with our destiny and their freedom is inextricably bound to our freedom. We cannot walk alone.*

The cadence of his words rolled over the crowd and electrified it. It swept over even the most diffident of journalists and soared over the assembled throng. And, then, came the words that have echoed for decades.

*I have a dream that my four children will one day live in a nation where they will not be judged by the color of their skin but by the content of their character.*

*I have a dream today.*

*I have a dream that one day the state of Alabama, whose governor's lips are presently dripping with the words of interposition and nullifi-*

*cation, will be transformed into a situation where little black boys and black girls will be able to join hands with little white boys and white girls and walk together as sisters and brothers.*

*I have a dream today.*

*I have a dream that one day every valley shall be exalted, every hill and mountain shall be made low, the rough places will be made plain, and the crooked places will be made straight, and the glory of the Lord shall be revealed, and all flesh shall see it together.*

*This is our hope. This is the faith with which I return to the South. With this faith we will be able to hew out of the mountain of despair a stone of hope. With this faith we will be able to transform the jangling discords of our nation into a beautiful symphony of brotherhood. With this faith we will be able to work together, to pray together, to struggle together, to go to jail together, to stand up for freedom together, knowing that we will be free one day.*

*This will be the day when all of God's children will be able to sing with a new meaning, "My country, 'tis of thee, sweet land of liberty, of thee I sing. Land where my fathers died, land of the pilgrim's pride, from every mountainside, let freedom ring."*

For myself and many, if not most, of the reporters gathered beside the Lincoln Memorial, there was a clear impression that we were seeing and hearing history being made. It has been said that journalism is the first rough draft of history. On this day, that draft needed very little polishing.

Just three months later, John F. Kennedy was assassinated and our world changed again.

I was on my way into work in Ft. Wayne when I noticed cars suddenly pulling off the road and stopping. It was as though some super magnetic force had halted traffic all around me. My first thought was that it was a *War of the Worlds* moment. I had no idea what had happened, but I swiftly turned on the radio which was set to 1190 on the dial and heard our news director Hal Cessna say, "This just in from the United Press. President Kennedy has been shot and killed in Dallas, Texas." All of us in the news department worked around the clock in an almost reflexive way for the next several days and many of those long hours still remain a blur. It was one of the very, very few times working in a news environment when absolutely no one displayed any of the black humor which often accompanies tragic or dramatic events.

Just a few months later, I received a call from WBBM – the CBS Owned & Operated station in Chicago – asking if I would be interested in working for them. Having grown up near Chicago, I did not hesitate. My answer was "Yes". So, once again, we packed our bags, called the movers and headed off to the Windy City. Chicago was then, and still is, a great place to work.

# CHAPTER 6

Having access to seats at Wrigley Field was a very definite perk that I – a lifelong Chicago Cubs fan – truly enjoyed. Richard Daley was mayor of the city and reporters had their own parking spaces at City Hall. Woe be unto any errant reporter who accidentally parked in the mayor's space. We even had flashing lights that we could use when rushing to the scene of a fire or a crime. If they also had issued us trench coats we could have provided a full cast for any movie about reporters. Actually, some of us did have trench coats but no movie roles. The Chicago political machine that Daley put together was everything that later legend said it was – effective, efficient and a bit corrupt. The same could be said of the Chicago police department at that time. It was not uncommon for a motorist who was pulled over for a traffic violation to hand the officer his driver's license with a twenty-dollar bill attached. The license would be returned and the infraction forgotten.

My stay in Chicago was relatively brief but included one memorable contact. Not long after arriving, I was assigned to interview Malcolm X who then was a major figure in the Nation of Islam which was headquartered in Chicago. Malcolm X was well known for his often fiery speeches, razor sharp criticism of whites and dynamic presence. It would be accurate to say that I was not warmly welcomed into his presence for the interview. Actually, the interview started out as something of a harangue, but I was persistent and respectful. Over the course of what turned out to be several interviews, we established a mutually respectful relationship. In fact, the better I got to know Malcolm X the better I liked him, and our conversations became more wide ranging. This was one very smart guy who rather clearly had ambitions of his own beyond just the Nation of Islam. And he never was boring.

Working at WBBM also brought my first contact with conservative icon Sen. Barry Goldwater. The Arizona senator was running for president against incumbent president Lyndon Johnson. I was assigned to cover his arrival at O'Hare airport for a campaign rally. Back then, candidates had little, if any, campaign entourage traveling with them and Goldwater got off the commercial flight carrying his own luggage. A controversy had been stirred up by some remarks he had made the day before. I do not recall the substance, but it was considered important at the time. Oddly enough, I was the only reporter waiting for Goldwater. So, as he came into the hallway, I waived my microphone, called out his name and started to ask the question at the top of my list. Very clearly, the senator wanted no part of it. Looking for a way to escape, he headed for the airport restroom. Unfortunately, he rushed into the women's restroom. Apparently, it was empty since no screams were heard and Goldwater, looking a bit sheepish, came back out, but he still refused to answer any questions.

Meanwhile, a friend of mine from the South Bend/Elkhart, Indiana, days had joined ABC News in New York. Bob Young had been both the news director and anchor at the ABC affiliate in South Bend and we had become friends during that period. After I moved to Chicago and he to New York, we continued to stay in touch by telephone. One day, he asked whether I would be interested in joining him at ABC. Wow! I never had been to New York and I was immediately intrigued. Bob said he would put me together with the head of ABC's radio news division and see where things went from there. So, I hopped a plane from Chicago and flew to New York to meet Tom O'Brien. Within minutes, it was clear that the job was mine, if I wanted it. However, O'Brien then turned to a radio sitting on a shelf behind him and switched it on, saying, "This is where I go for news". It was WNEW Radio and he suggested that I talk with them, even going so far as to arrange for me to meet with their news director Gerry Graham later that day.

WNEW was a legendary radio station. It is unlikely to this very day that there ever has been a radio station quite like it. Walking through that door in mid-town Manhattan was, for a broadcast journalist, the equivalent of a dancer walking through the door of the Radio City Music Hall. En route, I literally had collided with actor Sidney Poitier who was very gracious. I was thinking that I had been in New York for less than 24 hours and already had been up close and personal with a famous actor. As it turned out, celebrities were an ever day occurrence at WNEW.

Of course, the on-air staff was famous in its own right. The mornings started off with the comedy team of Gene Klaven and Dee Finch who had a strong following. Mid-day featured singer/songwriter Jim Lowe who was well known for the hits *Gambler's Guitar*

and *Behind the Green Door*. Jim and I became pals and used to try one-upping each other in a game of Name That Tune by picking songs off the jukebox at a nearby bar and correctly identifying them within the first five bars of music. Evenings belonged to golden voiced William B. Williams – host of the legendary *Make Believe Ballroom.*

Williams developed long running friendships with the top singers of the day – most of whom specialized in singing what came to be known as the Great American Songbook. These included Lena Horne and Nat King Cole. But his closest relationship was with Frank Sinatra who would come to the WNEW studios to record radio broadcasts. As the story goes, Williams observed one day that since Duke Ellington had been dubbed "The Duke" and Benny Goodman was known as "The King of Swing", then Sinatra should be called "Chairman of the Board." Of course, the title stuck and Sinatra became Williams' biggest fan. All of this added up to some interesting moments around the WNEW studios with Sammy Davis Jr. and Buddy Hackett and Mary Travers of Peter, Paul and Mary among the many performers who hung out there on a regular basis and often engaged us in idle chit chat. Mary was a news junky and spent a lot of time in the newsroom reading the wires which, in those days, included the Associated Press, United Press, International News Service and the British owned Reuters.

It is not an overstatement to say that the WNEW newsroom was outstanding, perhaps the very best in the business at that time and well beyond. In one year alone, it won the top three awards in broadcast journalism – the Ohio State Award, The Sigma Delta Chi Award and the Peabody. It routinely sent reporters to far distant lands to cover the important news of the day. Fans of the news operation included such famed broadcast news anchors as Walter Cronkite and Chet Huntley. The managing editor was gruff WWII veteran Jack Pluntze who demanded the best from his team every day. One day, I turned on a script just minutes short of deadline. He looked it over, declared it was "crap" and directed me to start writing again from the top. It was an impossible task and I looked up just about 5 minutes to air to discover that Jack had written a separate script on his own and was just teaching me a little humility,

The WNEW newsroom also was notorious for its addiction to puns. Some days, there was serious competition to see who could keep a pun going for as long as possible until someone finally ran out of words. I was delighted when I was able to slip this lead sentence past Jack on one newscast. It read "There is a new study out today that says the mothers of drug addicts are not necessarily heroines." Then, there was the horrible gaffe that occurred when a Pan American flight crashed in South America killing everyone aboard. The story broke just as the newscast was about to air and the newscast was sponsored by PanAm. Of course, the news anchor led with the plane crash and then went to commercial. We all cringed when the first line of the PanAm jingle went out over the airwaves declaring, "PanAm makes the going great!" However, the cringing was followed shortly by laughter. Black humor is a part of life in a newsroom.

1964 was an election year and Robert Kennedy was seeking to unseat Republican incumbent U.S. Senator Kenneth Keating. Despite their personal animosity, President Lyndon Johnson flew to New York to campaign for Kennedy and drew huge crowds. The New York Senate seat was very important, and the two men put aside their differences to improve the chances of a Democrat winning that seat. The breakthrough may well have come when Sen. Keating failed to show up for a debate with Kennedy shortly before the election. Kennedy debated an empty chair and soon after won the election. Debating an empty chair had a political history dating back to at least 1924 and it is certain that some on the Kennedy staff knew that history but what made this special was the fact that it was televised. The New York campaign also marked the start of my own relationship with RFK. Part of it may, in a sense, have had something to do with the fact that he and I were kind of the new kids in town. Kennedy, because he was not a native of New York, was called a "carpet bagger" by the Republicans and me because I was the kid from Indiana with his suitcase still packed.

In the meantime, I had stayed in touch with Malcolm X who also now was living in New York. Our occasional meetings were brief but friendly. I found him to be mellowing in his overall attitude toward whites and no longer referring to them generically as "devils".

He had travelled widely and read extensively and was well on his way to becoming a major figure in the black community. And he was brilliant. On February 21, 1965, I was en route to the famed Audubon Ballroom in Manhattan to cover a speech by Malcolm. I arrived just moments after a trio of assassins – believed to have been acting on behalf of the extremist Nation of Islam which Malcolm had left – had opened fire with a shotgun and pistols. People were still running from the ballroom and it took me a few moments to find out what had happened. Then, I got on our two-way radio in the car and called in to say that Malcolm X had been shot. I was the first reporter on the chaotic scene but none of us knew until a while later that he had been killed. I still believe that his death was a loss for all of us.

Meanwhile, I also got to know former President Herbert Hoover. He lived in an apartment in the famed Waldorf Astoria hotel in Manhattan and went for daily walks with just one security guard. I was sent out to get an interview with him and found him to be very accessible. Afterward, I made it a practice to stop by during some of his daily walks and listen to him talk about his days as president. Sometimes, we would sit on a sidewalk bench and chat. Much to my surprise, most of the time no one at all recognized him. Hoover firmly believed that he had done what was necessary while in office and he never really voiced any regrets. I do think that he genuinely enjoyed having a young reporter listen to him – not to do a story but just to listen.

Of course, there were those only in New York moments. Back when I was about 16, I had gone to the local movie theater in La Porte to see the new movie *The Pride & The Passion* starring Cary Grant, Frank Sinatra and Sophia Loren. I walked into the theater a couple of minutes late when the screen was showing a close up of Sophia Loren's eyes. I fell in love immediately. Now, jumping forward a few years, I was assigned to go out and interview Ms. Loren. I introduced myself to her public relations person and was sent directly over to start the interview. Ms. Loren greeted me warmly and I looked into her eyes and completely forgot every question I had planned to ask. I was speechless. This probably was not a new experience for Ms.

Loren because she graciously helped me get started with some questions, but I really don't remember a single word of the brief interview. However, I never have forgotten her eyes.

# CHAPTER 7

Everyone in the WNEW newsroom knew that my greatest passion when it came to reporting was politics. For me, the faintest whiff of a political story was like catnip to a cat. I had to have more. Nonetheless, I was stunned one morning when Gerry Graham called me into his newsroom office and asked me if I wanted to move to Washington, D.C. Robert Kennedy had won his race for the U.S. Senate and John Kluge – the multi-millionaire owner of the Metromedia Broadcasting chain which included WNEW as its flagship – had decided that Metromedia needed more of a presence in the nation's capital. Metromedia already owned television station WTTG on property near the border between Maryland and the District of Columbia and there was ample room in their building for a decent sized Washington Bureau. The company also owned radio and television stations in Philadelphia, Cleveland and Los Angeles, among others. My answer to Gerry's question was simple and direct. I said "yes". So, in the spring of 1965, my family – including wife Sue Ellen and both daughter Laura and baby daughter Lynne – packed our bags once more and we headed for the nation's capital.

I actually travelled to Washington a couple of weeks early just to get my feet on the ground and to do some house hunting. On my first day in town, I went up to the Capitol Building for the essential group tour which was very well done. Then I walked from there down to the mall with its large reflecting pond – a place I had not seen since I covered Martin Luther King's famous speech – and continued on to the Washington, Lincoln and Jefferson memorials and around the outside of the White House grounds before returning to my hotel where I pretty much collapsed. Even when you are young and in good shape, that is a pretty long hike.

Initially, Metromedia's Washington Bureau was fairly small. In addition to myself, there were reporters assigned to the State Department, White House, Pentagon and Capitol Hill, often rotating among assignments as the story or stories of the day warranted. Alan Walden oversaw national news coverage from New York. Fairly soon, though, we added Jack Laurence in Vietnam and would call upon the staff at WNEW for other assignments both in and out of the United States. Jack later joined CBS News and wrote a compelling book about his experiences in Vietnam. Our lineup of television and radio affiliates also expanded rapidly and before long we rivaled

CBS for the number of listeners reached on the radio side and our television outreach was growing, too.

Living on the outskirts of Washington offered my immediate family the opportunity to return more frequently to visit my parents in Indiana. Every time we crossed the Ohio-Indiana state line, we would burst into that favorite Hoosier song "Back Home Again in Indiana". Mostly, we did Indiana stuff – fishing at Tape Lake, which we owned, visiting relatives and just plain old hanging out.

Dad, Lynne, Mom, Laura, Me, Tom, Douglas

It rather quickly became clear that there were two places I much preferred to cover – Capitol Hill and the White House. These were the dual political hearts of the capital, along with a few bars and restaurants. Some of the best advice and insight I ever received came from two NBC News correspondents. I long had admired the reporting of Robert McCormick and Richard Harkness. Both men were veteran reporters and widely respected. On the first day that I walked into the Senate Radio and Television Gallery, I heard the very recognizable voice of McCormick booming from his small office at the rear of the gallery. I walked down the short corridor, poked my head in, introduced myself and declared how much I appreciated his reporting. He looked at me and said, "I have just one piece of advice for you, kid. Around here, keep your eyes and ears open and your mouth shut. You will learn a lot more that way." Over time, Bob and Dick took this young reporter under their wings, occasionally took me to lunch, and taught me how to count votes. Eventually, I came to be considered one of the most accurate vote counters covering the Senate. The key was to compare notes with the Senate staff members who were handling the respective pieces of legislation and then to factor in the informal counts made by the party whips and longtime Senate staff members. It took time and some care and feeding of egos among the key staff members. However, the end result was that I rarely miscounted a vote in advance. And I always appreciated the guidance of the veteran staffers.

In September of 1965, I was at the other end of Pennsylvania Avenue, in the White House press room with its ugly green couches, when we abruptly were summoned to the Oval Office for a meeting with President Johnson. He informed us – and, through us, the nation – that he would be going to the hospital for gall bladder surgery. A photo was snapped by a United Press photographer as we all scrambled for the door with our breaking news bulletin and there I was front and center. The La Porte Herald Argus ran the story on the front page and, much to my amusement, re-captioned the photo to declare that friends and acquaintances in La Porte were "startled" to see me in the crowd of reporters dashing out of the Oval Office.

Lyndon Johnson was very much a larger than life personality. At times, he seemed like a genuine force of nature – powerful and intimidating. Other times, he was almost playful. After one live broadcast of a news conference, LBJ quietly came up behind respected Westinghouse Broadcasting correspondent Sid Davis, who still was on the air live, and took over the microphone to tell listeners what a fine reporter Sid was. Most of us, Sid included, were flabbergasted. On another occasion, he stopped by the White House press lobby with its dilapidated green couches and came to an abrupt halt as he loomed over United Press International Audio Correspondent Pye Chamberlayne. Pye, an outstanding and occasionally brash reporter, was sound asleep. His head was wrapped in bandages because he had undergone a hair transplant. Johnson demanded – in a voice that probably could have been heard by people on Pennsylvania Avenue outside the White House – "What the hell are you people running here – a press corps infirmary?" His voice may or may not have been powerful enough to raise the dead, but it certainly raised Pye who sprang to his feet and stood at full attention while gasping out "It's the President. The President". Johnson probably was well aware of Pye's hair transplant and simply had seized the opportunity to ridicule Pye a bit. He then took a couple of questions from the rest of us and left the room.

The White House press corps accompanied Johnson on a state visit to what then was the West German capital of Bonn to attend the funeral of former Chancellor Konrad Adenauer. The visit took place during Octoberfest which meant that lots of Germans were partying like there would be no tomorrow. During a break in the official activities, NBC News anchor John Chancellor and I took a boat ride down the Rhine River and were captivated by the old mansions and castles that we saw along the way. For the most part, though, our schedule was hectic and made even more difficult by the time difference between Bonn and New York or Washington. When we left Bonn, we all thought we were going home. But Lyndon Johnson had other ideas. After we had been airborne for an hour, we were informed that the president would be making an impromptu visit to Ireland. While Johnson met with Irish officials at Shannon Airport, we were told that an agreement had been reached with Irish and American customs officials and that we had roughly an hour to visit the stores at the airport and do some shopping. All of us returned to our seats with bulging shopping bags. Once we were back in the air, another announcement was made to the effect that the Irish government also had loaded the plane with champagne and Irish whiskey which is the basic ingredient in Irish Coffee. By the time we finally landed at rainy Andrews Air Force Base outside Washington, none of us were feeling any pain. However, the spouses of some of us clearly were very pained by our condition as we staggered off the plane.

Just a few months later, many of us embarked on another trip – this one via a ship and, although Lyndon Johnson was not on board, he still was a participant. The National Governor's Association had decided to hold their annual convention in the territory of the United

States Virgin Islands – a collection of islands in the Caribbean administered respectively by the United States and Britain. This sea born gathering was dubbed almost immediately "The Ship of Fools", after a recent novel by Katherine Anne Porter. However, the voyage was anything but that.

In his book *Not a Ship of Fools*, author Albert Prendergast, observes, "Picture, if you will, the spectacle of all of the nation's governors, with their families and staffs, along with the cream of American journalism, representatives of the White House, well known members of the entertainment world, and the heads of major Fortune 500 companies embarking on a single ship for a voyage of over three-thousand miles of open sea to a small U.S. territory and return…

Terrorists were beginning their awful advance in many countries around the globe. And, to top off all of the lurking dangers, was the fact that the ship would be sailing into the Caribbean during the height of the hurricane season! In spite of all the drawbacks, the venture was a complete success." Of course, there were some special moments.

There had been increasing talk that two Republican governors – Nelson Rockefeller of New York and Ronald Reagan of California – might compete against each other for the GOP presidential nomination in 1968. Reporters looking for tea leaves to read found that the most interesting story was what appeared to be a developing friendship between the two governor's wives – Happy Rockefeller and Nancy Reagan. On many days, the two women could be found out on the deck of the Independence sitting side by side on the deck chairs. And they managed quite well to ignore the reporters hovering in the wings.

Meanwhile, the war in Vietnam continued to dominate much of the news, even while we were cruising down to the Virgin Islands. The governor of Texas at the time was Price Daniel who, of course, had ties to Lyndon Johnson. En route to the Virgin Islands, Daniel received a secret message from Johnson in the White House setting forth talking points in support of the war in Vietnam and directing Daniel to get as many of the governors as possible to back the

Administration's position. Somehow, that message fell into the hands of one of the top political managers on board the Independence and he – Lyn Nofziger – slipped the copy to me. I immediately realized that this was a good and quite unexpected news story. We already had made arrangements to transmit stories from ship to shore using single sideband radio links. I wrote the story, filed the report which I voiced to the Metromedia news desk in New York and shortly thereafter a political fire storm erupted. The New York Times and the Washington Post picked up the story and people were demanding to know how I had gotten my hands on a confidential White House communiqué. Naturally, I was not about to reveal my source. When we eventually returned to Washington, I was subpoenaed by a House of Representatives subcommittee and warned that, if I refused to answer their questions about my source, I would be held in contempt of Congress and go to jail. I responded that I would not say a word, packed my toothbrush and waited for the pending confrontation. Fortunately, cooler and wiser heads prevailed – I think from the White House – and the subpoena was dropped.

# CHAPTER 8

As noted earlier, I had developed a bit of a love affair with Capitol Hill. There were so many stories and so many issues and so many personalities. Both the House of Representatives and the Senate had their own special peculiarities. Although I spent more time on the Senate side than over at the House, there were tales to be told from both bodies. When I first arrived, the legendary Sam Rayburn, former Speaker of the House. still seemed to hover in the wings even though he had died in office a few years earlier. A gruff talking, outspoken, bourbon drinking Democrat Congressman from Texas, Rayburn was a master of the arcane rules of the House and could wield his considerable power with a sometimes heavy hand. There are many Rayburn stories, but my favorite involved his first meeting with a then youthful, newly elected Democrat from Hawaii – Daniel Inouye.

Inouye was a soft-spoken man who had been an authentic war hero during World War Two. While serving with the 442 Regiment in Italy, Inouye was seriously wounded leading an assault on a heavily-defended ridge. As he led his platoon, three German machine guns opened fire from covered positions just 40 yards away, Inouye stood up to attack and was shot in the stomach. Ignoring his wound, he attacked and destroyed the first machine gun. Despite being severely injured, Inouye rallied his men for an attack on the second machine gun position which he destroyed before collapsing from blood loss. Inouye was crawling toward the final bunker when a German inside fired a rifle grenade that struck him on the right elbow, severing most of his arm. As the German inside the bunker reloaded his rifle, Inouye managed to pry the live grenade from his useless right hand and transfer it to his left and tossed that grenade into the bunker, destroying it. He later was awarded the Medal of Honor.

When Inouye arrived on Capitol Hill, Speaker Rayburn followed the tradition of going down the lined up, newly elected Representatives and individually welcoming them to the House.

Rayburn worked his way down the line and eventually stood in front of then-Congressman Inouye. With typical modesty, Inouye tried to introduce himself, saying, "Mr. Speaker, I don't suppose who know who I am." Rayburn cut him off by responding, "I know who you are. How many one-armed Japs do you think we have in the House?" Inouye went on to be elected to the Senate, eventually becoming *president pro tem* of the Senate and thus third in the line of presidential succession after the Vice President and the Speaker of the House.

It was the Senate, however, that was home then to a number of extraordinary men and women. Among Democrats, there were Mike Mansfield, William Fulbright, Robert Kennedy, Ted Kennedy, Joseph Clark, Eugene McCarthy, George McGovern, John Glenn, Wayne Morse, Stuart Symington, Sam Irvin, Henry (Scoop) Jackson, Frank Church, William Proxmire, Phillip Hart, Birch Bayh, Walter Mondale and Fred Harris to name just a few. Among Republicans, Everett Dirksen, Margaret Chase Smith, Clifford Case, Jacob Javits, George Aikin, Tom Kuchel, John Sherman Cooper, Thruston Morton, Hugh Scott, John Tower, Peter Dominick, Charles Percy, Edward Brooke and Howard Baker among others. While there are tales I could tell about most of these men and women, all of whom were important sources of information for me at one time or another, I will make a serious effort to focus only on the highlights and, perhaps, on a couple of low lights. The hard part is deciding where to start.

J. William Fulbright was a senator from Arkansas and a remarkable person. He was the longest ever serving chairman of the Senate Foreign Relations committee. And, of course, he created the Fulbright scholarships that have benefited many students. He also was a segregationist.

He was a serious critic of the war in Vietnam and so infuriated Lyndon Johnson that the president began referring to him as Senator Halfbright. I covered many of his hearings on the war and on other matters and found him to be a relentless questioner with a solid grasp of the facts. Early on, I made it a point to introduce myself to him and ask for his insights. Over time, we developed an almost teacher-student relationship. After closed door briefings and hearings in the Foreign Relations Committee, Sen. Fulbright would wait until all the other reporters had left and only I remained. Then, he would open the door and beckon me inside. He would perch himself on the corner of his desk and tell me much of what had taken place behind those closed doors and give me his perspective on it. Since many of the hearings focused on Vietnam, Sen. Fulbright made it clear to me and, occasionally publicly, to others his great disdain for President Johnson. Often, it wasn't precisely what he said but the tone in his voice when he spoke about the president and Secretary of State Robert McNamara. The result of my private sessions with Fulbright frequently was an informed story that I was able to write with confidence in its accuracy. I never will forget his courtesy and kindness toward a very young reporter and his generosity with his time.

Then there was Everett McKinley Dirksen. The white haired Republican leader of the Senate was an extraordinary speaker. When he rose to speak on the Senate floor, an aide in the press gallery would shout out "Dirksen's up" and the gallery would empty as all of us rushed to listen to this amazing orator speak. Dirksen was a throwback to the early days of Senate speakers. He was in the mode of Henry Clay and William Jennings Bryan and others who could hold the Senate in their hands while they spoke. Listening to and watching Dirksen speak was like watching a performance on Broadway. He could reduce grizzled journalists to total silence as they became entranced by his words and his delivery. After speaking on the senate floor, he would come up to the press gallery where a bottle of either bourbon or scotch was kept in a drawer just for him. There, he would try to answer a host of serious or semi-serious questions humorously for half an hour before returning to his seat in the Senate chamber.

There was a connection, albeit slender, between Dirksen and my family on my mother's side. She was from Illinois, as was Dirksen, and a second cousin had held statewide office in Illinois. I unashamedly used that connection to introduce myself to Dirksen and he embraced me as a fellow Illinois friend, even though I was staunchly a Hoosier. Eventually, he began to invite me to join him for a drink. The drinks took place in the Minority Leader's office away from the Senate chamber. Our conversations stretched over several years and never were anything less than fascinating, at least from my perspective. Dirksen absolutely loved being a senator and felt honor bound to uphold the tradition of great speeches, good legislation and affection for his fellow members of the World's Most Exclusive Club.

This affection and concern was most evident when he asked me to deliver a message to Ted Kennedy. The young senator from Massachusetts had, at his father's request, submitted the name of Francis X. Morrissey to serve on the federal district court in Massachusetts. Opposition in the legal community and in the Senate was strong. Initially, Dirksen had been willing to let the nomination ride. But, as criticism of the choice increased, Dirksen saw the nomination headed for rejection. So, one afternoon while sitting in his private office, Dirksen said to me, "I know that you have a good relationship with the Kennedys and I would appreciate it if you would deliver a message to young Teddy from me. I like that young man but please tell him that the votes for confirmation are not there and I am going to speak out against the nomination." I agreed and did so that very afternoon, adding my own assessment that this was a fight not worth having. Robert Kennedy shared that view and the nomination was withdrawn. Of course, I also took advantage of my information to break the story that the Morrissey nomination would be dropped much like the hot potato it had become.

John Glenn was the first American to orbit the Earth and the fifth person in space, after cosmonauts Yuri Gagarin and Gherman Titov and fellow Mercury Seven astronauts Alan Shepard and Gus Grissom. Glenn was a combat pilot in the Marine Corps and one of the Mercury Seven astronauts, who were the elite U.S. military test pilots selected by the National Aeronautics & Space Administration to operate the experimental Mercury spacecraft and become the first American astronauts. He flew the Friendship 7 mission on February 20, 1962. In 1965, Glenn retired from the military and resigned from NASA so he could be eligible to stand for election to public office. As a member of the Democratic Party he was elected to represent Ohio in the U.S. Senate and also ran briefly for president.

John and I and his indomitable wife Annie, who had overcome a severe stuttering problem, became friends over the course of dinners and other events at Hickory Hill, the home of Robert and Ethel Kennedy, as well as on the campaign trail. He always was a straight shooter and a thorough good guy. Nonetheless, during his short run for the Democratic presidential nomination, I pursued a line of questions that he felt was unreasonable and he slammed his car door in my face. The next day we both apologized and our relationship remained unchanged. John's press secretary at the time was a young man named Mike McCurry who went on to work for a number of prominent Democrats, including Bill Clinton when he was president. To this day, I consider Mike to be one of the best press secretaries to work for any elected official.

A favorite of most reporters was George Aikin, a Republican senator from Vermont. Many of us believed that Aikin and Senate Majority Leader Mike Mansfield must have been separated at birth. Both specialized in very short answers to questions – no matter how long the question. "Yep" and "Nope" were their favorite words. Nonetheless, both were very approachable. Perhaps not always informative but approachable. Both men were critics of the Vietnam War and Aikin offered a way out. He said, "We should just declare victory and go home." Many applauded that suggestion.

Since WNEW was the flagship station for the Metromedia network, I periodically was reminded that my job included paying attention to the two senators from New York. The senior senator was Republican Jacob Javits who was a product of New York City's notorious Lower East Side. That background instilled in him a strong work ethic and a genuine concern for people less fortunate. He clearly was among the smartest members of Congress and his political skills were the stuff of legend. One day, he and I were standing on the marble steps of the Senate when a couple approached and somewhat timidly introduced themselves, telling Sen. Javits that they were from a very small town in upstate New York and innocently suggesting that Javits may not even know the town existed. Javits immediately set them at ease, telling them that not only was he familiar with their small town, but he knew some of their neighbors – mentioning names of people the couple knew. By the time Javits finished chatting with the couple you would have thought they were long lost relatives. I indicated to Javits that I was impressed that he was so familiar with the small town. His reply summed it up for me as he said, "Of course I know that town and its people. I am their senator."

Robert Kennedy was the other senator from New York. His Senate staff was filled with very bright, hardworking people who were fiercely loyal to their boss and committed to making a difference in the world. Among the standouts were Peter Edelman and Adam Walinsky – two brilliant young firebrands who sometimes got out ahead of Kennedy on some issues. Then there were the two definite grown-ups –Chief of Staff Joe Dolan and Press Secretary Frank Mankiewicz. Both men had remarkable senses of humor, great skill in managing people and extraordinary closeness with Robert Kennedy that allowed them to anticipate what he might want or need and then get it done. They were the go to guys and being around them was a bit like taking a masters course in a very special school.

I soon learned that one of the best times to catch Kennedy for an interview or conversation was near the end of the day. So, when necessary, I would park myself in the anteroom to his office and just wait. Once, when he walked out, he stopped and declared, "You have to be the most patient reporter I've ever met." I was not sure whether that was faint praise or condemnation, but I continued to practice patience.

Kennedy, himself, was not widely known for his patience, although he tried hard occasionally to at least appear patient. At one point, he and Senator Carl Curtis of Nebraska both attended a Senate committee hearing at which auto safety activist Ralph Nader testified. Curtis repeatedly interrupted Nader's testimony, beginning most of his questions with the phrase, "Mr. Nader, I do not understand…." After several of these interruptions, Kennedy's patience gave out. Curtis again interrupted and Kennedy leaned into the microphone to ask "words of more than one syllable?" It took many observers great effort to keep from bursting into laughter. Curtis, whom any reporters referred to as "piglet" from the Winnie the Pooh books, shared the Senate with his Nebraska colleague Roman Hruska. A staunch conservative and much more respected than Curtis, Hruska became best known for a statement that did not reflect his abilities. President Nixon had nominated Judge G. Harold Carswell for a seat on the U.S. Supreme Court. Early on, it was clear that Carswell was a mediocre candidate and not of Supreme Court caliber. During an interview in the Senate press gallery, Hruska infamously declared, "Even if he were mediocre, there are a lot of mediocre judges and people and lawyers. They are entitled to a little representation, aren't they, and a little chance?" The stunned silence that greeted that remark was impressive.

Fairly early in Kennedy's term, the Transit Union went on strike in New York City. It was the first major strike since the founding of the Transit Workers and it lasted for twelve bitter days. Union leaders repeatedly told me that if Kennedy would talk with them they would listen and be inclined to end their walkout. Kennedy, however, steadfastly kept his distance from the strike. As the strike wore on, I wrote a story essentially saying that the strike could be shortened if only Kennedy would pick up the phone and talk with the union leadership. The story was sharply critical of Kennedy and he heard about it. A day later, I was walking down the Senate steps when I saw Kennedy coming the other way. I fully expected one of his well-known icy stares. He stopped and said, "Dan, did you have to say what you said in that story?" And I replied, "Yes. Senator, I did." He looked at me for a moment and then nodded. The subject never came up again.

Indeed, Kennedy and I continued to have a warm relationship, as I also did with members of his staff. Over time, I and sometimes my family began being invited to dinners and parties at Hickory Hill, the Kennedy home. I quickly learned that Ethel Kennedy was fiercely protective of both her husband and the growing number of children that made up the family. Being invited to their home often was like stepping into a human whirlwind. And it was great fun. As mentioned earlier, this was where John Glenn and I became friends, as well as singer Andy Williams, mountaineer Jim Whittaker and, of course, Ted Kennedy. Hays Gorey, a terrific reporter for Time Magazine, also was a frequent guest, as was columnist Art Buchwald and a handful of other journalists.

One year, at the annual pet competition, our dog – a Springer Spaniel – took the blue ribbon and made us all proud. On another occasion, they had a press-celebrity tennis tournament and I actually got to play with tennis greats Stan Smith and Arthur Ashe. To say that I was thrilled is an understatement. Among a number of other occasions, there is one that remains firmly in my memory. It was a Hallowe'en party. The Kennedys had a couple of dogs – one of which was a giant black Newfoundland named Brumus. Most of the time, Brumus was a gentle giant but everyone knew there were some things you simply did not do such as putting your hand on RFK's car – especially if RFK was in it. It would be a good way to lose a hand. In the case of the Hallowe'en party, Brumus was sprawled on the floor by the front door doing his best to be immune to the young partiers swirling around him. However, there came a moment when someone rang the doorbell and Ethel swung the door open. A very young trick or treater stood on the doorstep. At that moment, Brumus decided to yawn. His giant jaws opened wider and wider like a cavernous maw. The child stood transfixed for a moment, then let out a scream and took off running. Brumus, looking bemused, never moved and several of us rushed to reassure the frightened child and parent that the giant dog was not going to eat anyone. Soon, calm was restored but I remember that moment to this day.

I would be very remiss if I did not mention longtime Kennedy staff member and family spokeswoman Melody Miller. The word remarkable falls short of really describing her. Blonde, brilliant, articulate, politically savvy, media-wise and loyal, Melody became a friend and confident and eventually my son Dylan's godmother. If ever necessary, I would turn to her for insight, advice and comfort over the years. She truly is a legend in Washington and her list of friends and admirers may be longer than those of some presidents.

In January of 1967, Kennedy decided to make a whirlwind tour of part of Europe. The trip included stops in England, Paris, Germany and Italy. I was invited to go along as was ABC News correspondent Bob Clark. Metromedia executives decided it was a good idea for me to accept the invitation and so I did. The fourth person on the trip was longtime Kennedy friend Bill vanden Heuval – a former assistant to RFK when he was Attorney General. Bob Clark, an outstanding veteran reporter, and I both spoke French, but I have no idea whether that influenced our selection.

The trip was dominated mostly by questions from almost everyone about the Vietnam War and Kennedy's evolving position on it. Clearly, his opposition was growing as was reflect in remarks he made at the famous Oxford Union which was one of his first stops on the trip. Asked about the war, Kennedy expressed "grave reservations" but deflected any other questions. The next stop was Paris where Kennedy met briefly with President Charles de Gaulle. But it was the next meeting with Etienne Manac'h, director of Far Eastern Affairs for the French Foreign Office. Manac'h offered up what he described as a three-point plan that could move Vietnam toward some peaceful settlement. Kennedy – who did not speak French but listened to a simultaneous translation – did not feel he had heard anything new and was inclined, in any case, to be cautious about making foreign policy pronouncements while abroad. At that point, I dropped off the trip when an embassy doctor grounded me with a diagnosis of pneumonia.

When RFK and I both arrived back in the United States, on separate flights, both he and I were stunned to see a story in Newsweek and the New York Times saying that Kennedy had received a "peace feeler" from the North Vietnamese. Kennedy was surprised because he was not aware of any such peace feeler and I was equally surprised because, as a reporter traveling with him, I had no sense of any peace feeler either from English or French speaking officials and Paris-based reporters. As it turned out, there was not one but the reports resulted in a widely publicized and highly confrontational meeting at the White House between Kennedy and Lyndon Johnson.

The year was to be heavily influenced by events surrounding the war in Vietnam. Protests were growing throughout the United States and Defense Secretary Robert McNamara resigned when his proposal for a halt to the bombing of North Vietnam and turning the fighting over the South Vietnamese was rejected. Speculation grew that Robert Kennedy would oppose President Johnson's re-election in 1968 but he consistently said he would not run. Kennedy's insistence that he would not be a candidate prompted another senator of Irish heritage to take the plunge instead.

# CHAPTER 9

## *The 1968 Campaign*

On November 30th, Minnesota Senator Eugene McCarthy announced that he would challenge Lyndon Johnson for the 1968 Democratic presidential nomination. McCarthy was essentially a back bencher in the Senate but popular with many liberal Democrats for his unstinting criticism of the Vietnam War and the Johnson Administration's policies. His caustic wit often was directed at other politicians, including other members of the Senate, and his disdain for the Kennedy family was well known. His major complaint seemed to be that they were not intellectual enough. Reporters often went to McCarthy for a quote when they were looking for something with some bite to it. A classic example is a comment he made about Michigan Governor George Romney who was seeking the Republican presidential nomination.

Romney – a well-regarded governor and a very decent man – had developed some reservations about the Vietnam War. He made a personal trip to Vietnam to meet with U.S. military leaders in the country and was given a series of briefings. He returned saying that he supported the war effort. However, it was clear that the support was somewhat less than enthusiastic. During a campaign appearance in New Hampshire, Romney reversed himself and declared that he had been "brainwashed" by the military during his trip to Vietnam. In political circles, Romney's comment was referred to as the "great brain robbery" – borrowing from a movie titled "The Great Train Robbery". Asked by several of us outside the Senate dining room what he thought about Romney's change of position, Sen. McCarthy said he thought the great brain robbery actually was "more like petty theft." Romney's presidential campaign ended shortly after. McCarthy's presidential bid gathered steam.

The McCarthy campaign was not well funded and depended heavily on the work of young volunteers who were guided by a very small core of experienced political activists. These included Allard Lowenstein, Seymour Hersch and Mary Louise Oates. Hersch and Oates went on to become respected journalists. The McCarthy campaign often was referred to as the "Children's Crusade" because so many young people who passionately opposed the Vietnam War and the draft volunteered to help. They shaved their beards, combed their hair, threw out some of their drugs and became "neat and clean for Gene." In fact, the young volunteers often were the focus of news stories about the McCarthy campaign.

At best, Sen. McCarthy was a diffident campaigner much as he had been a somewhat diffident senator. His speeches often tended to be more poetic than political and he enjoyed displaying his intellectual accomplishments more than he enjoyed dealing with the politics of a presidential campaign. Nonetheless, he offered a clear alternative to Johnson and the conduct of the Vietnam war. One early result was that in March of 1968 Johnson conceded the state of Massachusetts to McCarthy which gave him 72 convention delegates. But McCarthy's main focus was on the state of New Hampshire where I joined the traveling campaign press corps to see how things would play out in the Granite State.

To the surprise of almost everyone, McCarthy won 42.2% of the New Hampshire vote, falling just 7 points short of Lyndon Johnson's total. The result widely was regarded as a "moral" victory for McCarthy and added new energy to his campaign. But it also changed the dynamics of the 1968 campaign. On March 16th, as McCarthy and the accompanying reporters, including myself, flew back to Washington, Robert Kennedy announced that he would enter the presidential race, too.

McCarthy, many of his supporters – some of whom had pushed for a Kennedy candidacy but grew tired of waiting – and even some reporters were either dismayed or angered by Kennedy's late decision to enter the fray. For me, it meant that the election had become a three-man contest between Kennedy, McCarthy and Johnson and that I would be shuttling back and forth between the Kennedy and McCarthy campaigns. The Johnson campaign would be covered by the White House team.

Perhaps nothing so reflects the dynamic that led Robert Kennedy to change his mind and enter the presidential primary campaign than a quote from Shakespeare's Julius Caesar. In Act IV, Scene 3, in which the author wrote:

> There is a tide in the affairs of men
> Which, taken at the flood, leads on to fortune;
> Omitted, all the voyage of their life
> Is bound in shadows and in miseries.
> On such a full sea are we now afloat;
> And we must take the current when it serves,
> Or lose our ventures.

I always have thought that RFK saw the direction of the tide and decided to follow it, even though the tide was already running ahead of him.

Certainly, his first campaign foray to the state of Kansas allayed some concerns about his late entry into the race. He made what I considered to be trial runs through appearances at Kansas State and Kansas universities where some thought that he might face harsh criticism from the residents of Middle America. On March 18th, he stopped first at Kansas State where the field house was packed with more than 14,500 people, including some McCarthy supporters and Kennedy critics. However, Kennedy received thunderous ovation after ovation that left my ears ringing. Then, it was on to the University of Kansas where an estimated 17,000 people turned out and their responses were even more emotional than at Kansas State. I think a lot of us in the traveling press corps – myself included – could have summed up or response with a single word – "Wow!" But, of course, one word will never be enough for a group of writers and so many more words followed.

I continued to shuttle between the Kennedy and McCarthy campaigns – the former often flying on the wings of euphoria because of the huge and enthusiastic crowds it drew. At the same time, I was aware that an important date was approaching. March 28th was the deadline for filing to take part in the Indiana primary which was scheduled of May 7th. Back in Washington, I joined Bob and his brother Ted on the steps of the Capitol to talk about Indiana. Both of them knew that I was a native Hoosier with continuing ties to the state, including connections with senior senator Vance Hartke and with Sen. Birch Bayh, a personal friend. Indiana's governor – Roger Brannigan – would be on the ballot as a stand-in for Lyndon Johnson and Eugene McCarthy already had filed papers to be on the ballot. We talked for some length and I raised some possible negatives – noting the state's inherent conservatism and the power of the well-funded political machine supporting Brannigan. However, I also pointed out that the northern tier of the state tended to be more liberal and more Democratic, as did some of the college towns, including South Bend which is home to Notre Dame and that the state had sent two liberal Democrats to the Senate. Ted continued to sound cautiously pessimistic, but I could see that Bob wanted to run in Indiana as a test of his strength against McCarthy. Although no immediate decision was made, I walked away thinking that I would be visiting my home state with the Kennedy campaign.

Meanwhile, I was traveling with the McCarthy campaign in Waukesha, Wisconsin, near the end of March when Lyndon Johnson went on national television on March 31st to announce that he would not seek re-election. One of our traveling press colleagues volunteered to watch the Johnson speech expecting, as we all did, that it would involve an increase in U.S. troop strength in Vietnam. He was breathless as he rushed back to tell us that Johnson would not run. A McCarthy aide literally interrupted McCarthy's speech on stage to tell the senator what Johnson had said. Then, we stormed the stage to get McCarthy's reaction. He seemed more than a little stunned and unusually short on words. He quickly left the stage and returned to his hotel room to assess what had occurred. McCarthy acknowledged that the race temporarily had become one between himself and Robert Kennedy and added that while he was not "seeking a knockdown, drag-out battle" neither was he "seeking an accommodation." He also assumed, as we all did, that Vice President Hubert Humphrey soon would enter the contest. And, indeed, shortly thereafter he did.

# CHAPTER 10

On April 4th, Kennedy traveled to Indianapolis for a planned speech in the city's black wards. As the plane took off for Indianapolis, word came that Dr. Martin Luther King had been shot. On arrival at the Indianapolis airport, it was confirmed that Dr. King had been killed. However, it appeared that no one in the large crowd that was waiting for Kennedy had been told about the shooting. So, it fell to the candidate to break the news which he did and followed up with an extraordinary and heart felt speech that included the rare mention of his own loss when President Kennedy was assassinated. He urged the people in the crowd to go home and pray for the King family. Then, he concluded, *"Let us dedicate ourselves to what the Greeks wrote so many years ago: to tame the savageness of man and to make gentle the life of this world. Let us dedicate ourselves to that and say a prayer for our country and for our people."* It may have been in that moment that many of us thought we were seeing what the future of America might hold were Robert Kennedy to become president.

The presidential campaigns suspend their activity for a few days and I returned to Washington to see firsthand the results of the violence that had erupted in some cities across the country. Perhaps the most stunning was the sight of machine gun emplacements on the grounds of the U.S Capitol Building. It was as though the government felt itself under attack and feared the violence that might follow. There also were broken windows in some parts of town and looting of some stores. Soon, however, sanity or exhaustion prevailed. And Robert Kennedy returned to Indiana.

There were a lot of campaign stops to come in Indiana but two stand out in my mind for what will be obvious reasons. The first was a speech at Purdue University from which I had graduated in 1961. As he began to speak, RFK gestured to me. I was standing in the wings to take notes when he stunned me by telling the capacity crowd in the Edward C. Elliott hall of music that he was traveling with a Purdue graduate – Dan Blackburn – who had just been selected as one of the Outstanding Young Men in America. The crowd applauded and I was flabbergasted but also thrilled. I only had learned of the honor a few weeks earlier, presumably as a result of being nominated by Purdue. However, that is only a guess as they did not disclose the source of nominations. The second came a few weeks later in my home town of La Porte.

On May 6, 1968, The Kennedy campaign rolled from South Bend, the home of Notre Dame, to La Porte, Indiana. Along the way, road signs that had been advertising that Kennedy would pass by – "Robert Kennedy will be here today" were replaced with new ones in La Porte County saying that Kennedy would be there accompanied by Dan Blackburn. The signs were the inspiration of Dick Tuck – a Kennedy advance man known for his puckish humor as well as his aggressiveness. Dick had a strong dislike for Richard Nixon and bedeviled the Nixon campaign repeatedly, at one point donning a conductor's hat and directing the engineer on the Nixon campaign train to pull out of the station before Nixon finished speaking. Eventually, Dick ran for election in San Francisco with the slogan "The job needs Tuck and Tuck needs the job" He lost and promptly declared, "The people have spoke; the bastards." Back in La Porte, with my parents in the audience, Kennedy playfully described me in terms that would have been more appropriate for a Pulitzer Prize winner. Then, we headed west toward Gary.

It was an amazing afternoon. Enthusiastic crowds lined the streets and the sides of the connecting highways by the thousands. Along the way, we all noticed two young women waving at Kennedy and jumping up and down and then running to their car to get ahead of us. Over the next few hours, the women were spotted at least 13 times, until, finally, the photographers in the open car behind

Kennedy asked the young women to hop in, which they did. There is no word on how or whether they eventually retrieved their car. As the sun set, the motorcade rolled on through the towns of Gary and Hammond. A speech had been scheduled to take place in Whiting which sits on the Indiana-Illinois border. The speech had been set for 5:00pm. Our slow-moving motorcade arrived after 10:00pm. From there, it was on to Indianapolis – fortunately by plane.

There is another Indiana campaign anecdote. Two days before the incredible motorcade across the northern edge of the state, Kennedy made an appearance at Valparaiso University where he spoke and took some questions. I ducked into an office on the university campus to call in a report to our assignment desk in New York. However, I missed Kennedy delivering the get-to-the-bus tagline of his speeches – *"As George Bernard Shaw once said, some men see things as they are and ask why. I dream things that never were and ask why not."* That was the signal to reporters to get ready to leave. So, when I came out of the campus office, the bus was gone. I knew I had to get to the airport before the campaign plane took off. A college student in a hot rod was driving by and I flagged him down and said that, if he could get me to the plane before it took off, I would give him twenty dollars. The student drove like a mad man. As we pulled onto the tarmac, the plane was starting to taxi. Frank Mankiewicz and Bill Barry were leaning out an open door urging us on. We matched speed with the plane rolling down the runway. I stood up. Frank and Bill shouted "Jump!" I did and they caught me by the arms and pulled me into the plane. As they closed the door, I looked down and there, clutched in my hand, was the twenty-dollar bill that I had promised to the driver of the hot rod. At least, he had a heckuva story to tell.

And still more from Indiana. The Kennedy campaign rented a five-car diesel train to do some old-fashioned campaigning by train starting in Logansport and following along the tracks made famous by the song Wabash Cannonball. Having little else to do, traveling reporters wrote a seven-stanza song about the campaign titled The Ruthless Cannonball taking note of RFK's alleged ruthlessness. The first verse went "*Oh listen to the speeches that baffle, beef and bore, As he waffles through the woodlands and slides along the shore. He's the politician who's touched by one and all. He's the demon driver of The Ruthless Cannonball.* And on it went as the press corps serenaded the candidate and his wife both of whom responded by applauding when the song reached its end.

Kennedy went on to win the Indiana primary with 42% of the vote and, without pausing, was on to Nebraska for the next go round. However, the dynamic changed as McCarthy decided essentially to take a pass on the Cornhusker state and move ahead to Oregon and California. President Johnson's name still was on the Nebraska ballot because his withdrawal had come too late to have it removed. And Hubert Humphrey was campaigning. Still, Kennedy seemed more relaxed in this state where increasingly he was favored to win. On one of the campaign swings, the Kennedy bus stopped in the town of Wahoo, Nebraska, much to the delight of traveling reporters who wanted to use that address as the dateline for their stories. The local theater had a sign promoting the current movie. It was "The Happiest Millionaire" and a smiling Kennedy told the crowd,

"I hope that is what you will make me tomorrow" – primary election day. As expected, Kennedy won and by more of a margin than predicted – 51.5% to McCarthy's 31%. Humphrey and Johnson were in single digits.

Next up was Oregon to be followed by California – both important states. It was decided that I would switch over mostly to McCarthy in Oregon where his chances looked good and move back to the Kennedy campaign in California afterward. Oregon was a strongly anti-Vietnam war state and Eugene McCarthy had a head start in wooing the voters there. It quickly became obvious that this time the contest would be an uphill effort for Kennedy and McCarthy seemed more relaxed and confident than he had in the earlier states. As the McCarthy campaign flew from one small airport to another, we suddenly had an unexpected to close call. As we were taking off from one airport, a plane approached head-on for a landing. Both pilots veered sharply away from each other and the planes missed colliding by several feet. However, all of us on board were seriously holding our breaths. Over the course of the few days in Oregon, McCarthy disparaged Kennedy supporters as less intelligent and less well-educated. He also referred to my home state of Indiana disdainfully saying, "They keep talking about the poet out there. I asked if they were talking about Shakespeare or even my friend Robert Lowell. But it was James Whitcomb Riley. You could hardly expect to win under those conditions."

In the following days, McCarthy became more aggressive much to the delight of his supporters. McCarthy called Kennedy a symbol of the old politics not new politics. Both he and Kennedy had scheduled tours of the Portland Zoo and, coincidentally, at roughly the same time. When told of McCarthy's approach, Kennedy jumped into a waiting convertible and raced away. By doing so, he left the bus full of traveling reporters waiting and McCarthy climbed onto the bus and suggested that all the reporters should switch to covering his campaign. As the results came in on election night, McCarthy rolled to an impressive 44.7% to Kennedy's 38.8%. McCarthy was euphoric, declaring "We'll take the fence down around the White House and have a picnic on the lawn." He also shouted, "California here we come." Bill Rosendahl, a campaign worker in Oregon who went on to become a TV host and Los Angeles City Councilman, had the unenviable task of informing RFK that he had lost that state. The next day I headed back to the Kennedy campaign.

For any presidential candidate, campaigning in California is very much like campaigning in a nearby nation. The sprawling state was then and still is widely diverse. Even in 1968, however, Los Angeles County was especially important to the Kennedy campaign because of its significant number of black and Hispanic voters. In addition, it was and remains a very media centric state and getting your face on television and voice on the radio played a very important role in campaign strategy. Kennedy's relationship with United Farm Workers leader Cesar Chavez was a definite asset. The California campaign was headed by the powerful state legislator Jesse Unruh who sometimes seemed like a force of nature. In addition, Kennedy brother-in-law Steve Smith also moved into the Los Angeles campaign headquarters who essentially provided very clear direction to all involved. Steve was the Irish equivalent of a consigliere and thoroughly trusted by all the Kennedys. In addition, Frank Mankiewicz – a native Californian—knew how to reach out to a wide range of supporters and add them to the celebrity speaker roster. The first thing Kennedy did after arriving in California from the Oregon loss was to offer up the possibility of a debate with Eugene McCarthy. Faced with a crowd of reporters, Kennedy conceded that the Oregon loss had damaged his campaign and that he was not the same candidate that he had been before the Oregon primary. He pulled up an old quote from Abraham Lincoln when asked by someone—possibly me—how it felt to be the first Kennedy to lose a campaign. Kennedy described Lincoln picturing a man being run out of town on a rail and declaring, "If it were not for the honor of the thing I'd rather have walked." It was a classic Kennedy moment.

In the background, another sentiment was underway among many of us covering the campaign. Several veteran reporters including such tough guys as Dick Harwood – an ex-Marine working for the Washington Post and someone highly critical of Kennedy when he joined the campaign – and Time Magazine's Hays Gorey, ABC's Bob Clark and others all had tentatively decided to drop off the campaign after the California primary. I had made a similar decision. The reason was simple. We all had come to like the candidate too much and wanted him to win the Democratic nomination. Maintaining objectivity was increasingly difficult. I believe Jules Witcover, one of the best political reporters of the last several decades, also had reached that tipping point. For a group of presumably hard-nosed reporters, it was an extraordinary development.

Meanwhile, the motorcade headed for downtown Los Angeles with Olympic Decathlon Champion Rafer Johnson joining Bill Barry at Kennedy's side. It was South Bend to Gary all over again with thousands of cheering supporters crowding the streets and with little control from the Los Angeles police department because Mayor Sam Yorty was openly hostile to Kennedy. There was one more train ride to come – a whistle-stop tour up California's Central Valley. Then, it was on to San Francisco and a debate with Gene McCarthy. And there the atmosphere had darkened after McCarthy released a commercial that seriously distorted Kennedy's record on Vietnam and attempted to tie him to the 1965 Johnson Administration's involvement in the Dominican Republic even though Kennedy was not part of the Johnson Administration then. The mutual dislike between Kennedy and McCarthy was growing more visible.

The Kennedy campaign returned once more to San Francisco on June 3rd, logging some 1200 miles between Los Angeles, San Francisco, Long Beach, San Diego and back to Los Angeles—a thoroughly exhausting day mostly dominated by a stop in San Francisco's Chinatown where half a dozen sharp explosions – similar to gunshots – rang out. Kennedy did not even flinch and the sharp sounds turned out to be firecrackers. The last poll of the California campaign showed Kennedy leading with 36% to 31% for McCarthy and a slender 15% for a slate supporting Hubert Humphrey. However, 18% were undecided which was worrisome to members of the Kennedy staff.

Election Day always is a time to catch your breath, get some rest and wait and wait and wait. Everything that can be done has been done. The Kennedy family headed to the Malibu home of director John Frankenheimer where the beach beckoned. There was a tense moment when young David Kennedy was pulled beneath the waves by the undertow. However, the candidate immediately dove in to rescue his son and, except for a few bumps and bruises, all was well.

At the Ambassador Hotel, many of us were running through our various checks with producers, phone lines and all the small details that make live broadcasts come together. My friend Bob Clark from ABC was doing the same thing at his desk next door. Upstairs, members of the Kennedy family, close aides and a handful of reporters gathered to wait for the polls to close and the results to come in. Earlier in the day, Kennedy had won the South Dakota primary with 49.7% of the vote. Exit polling suggested a similar trend in California. By now, it was clear that Kennedy would win California. I was among those in the fifth-floor suite. Ethel Kennedy was bouncing up and down on a bed – the excitement of the moment energizing her. I sat down with RFK to do an interview – as it turned out his last such interview. It was relatively straight forward. He talked about looking forward to the Democratic convention in Chicago where he expected to be nominated. I asked whether he thought that he and McCarthy might be able to bury the hatchet and he said that he hoped they would. Privately, I thought it more likely that McCarthy would try to bury the political hatchet in RFK. Then, moments later we all squeezed into the elevator going down to the first floor near the Embassy Ballroom where throngs of supporters had packed the entire area. The atmosphere was electric with excitement and anticipation.

After touching on several of the key campaign issues, a smiling Robert Kennedy began to wrap things up and he did so with praise for his campaign workers. "I thank all of you who made this possible this evening. All of the effort that you made and all of the people whose places I haven't been to, but who made or did all of the work at the precinct level, got out the vote, did all the efforts, brought forth all of the efforts required. I was a campaign manager eight years ago and I know what a difference that kind of commitment can make. My thanks to all of you and on to Chicago." – A reference to the planned site of the Democratic National Convention.

I had worked my way up to the stage and planned to follow the Kennedy team to a second location where he would meet with some local officials before going on to a party at the Factory – a Los Angeles night spot. However, the Kennedy team suddenly detoured back toward the kitchen because it seemed like an easier, less congested route. Still following, I suddenly heard a series of popping noises. Having grown up in a part of the country where guns and sport shooting remain common, I knew that what I heard were gunshots and not balloons bursting. Immediately, I spun around and raced back to our broadcast location. We still had our lines up and I called the desk in New York to alert them that I heard shots being fired and to get us back on the air. Within a handful of minutes, we were back live – the first to do so. Shortly thereafter, Kennedy in-law Steve Smith arrived on stage and appealed for a doctor – asking repeatedly that if a doctor was present would he or she come forward. It became clear that Robert Kennedy had been shot. Later, I learned that United Auto Workers official Paul Schrade – a friend over the years – also had been shot in the head. Eventually, he recovered.

The scene soon shifted to Good Samaritan Hospital where Kennedy had been transported after initial emergency treatment. He now was in the intensive care unit on the hospital's 5th floor. Frank Mankiewicz began providing occasional briefings for all of us waiting in a makeshift press area. Early in the morning, he announced that surgery had been completed and that all but one fragment of a bullet had been removed. However, he added that while RFK was breathing on his own, "There may have been an impairment of the blood supply to the midbrain which doctors explained as governing certain of the vital signs – heart, eye track, level of consciousness – although not directly the thinking process." Shortly afterward, Eugene McCarthy stopped by the hospital and announced that he was suspending his own campaign for the presidency. As evening approached, signs appeared outside the hospital reading "Pray for Bobby". Frank Mankiewicz appeared again to tell the assembled members of the press corps that, "As of now, Senator Kennedy's condition is still described as extremely critical as to life." As the night dragged on toward morning, few, if any, among us had any doubts that the end was near. Then, at 2:00 A.M., an exhausted Frank Mankiewicz appeared once more. He said, "I have a short announcement to read at this time. Senator Robert Francis Kennedy died at 1:44 A.M. today, June 6, 1968. With Senator Kennedy at the time of his death were his wife, Ethel; his sisters Mrs. Stephen Smith and Patricia Lawford, brother-in-law Stephen Smith and Mrs.

John F. Kennedy." At that point, Hayes Gorey of Time Magazine and I stepped up, put our arms around Frank and walked him off the stage to prevent any further questions. Then, once again, plans were started for the laying to rest of another Kennedy and another presidential plane was sent to take his body and family members to New York where a Solemn Requiem Mass would be held in the magnificent St. Patrick's Cathedral to be followed by burial in Arlington National Cemetery not far from the grave of his older brother.

The traveling press corps and some staff members flew back together to New York. Some of us slept. Most of us wrote various versions of obituaries and even reminiscences. The plane was unusually quiet as we all sought to absorb what really had happened. Most of us firmly believed that we had lost someone who would have led us to a newer and better world. Many of us believe it to this very day.

Here is what I wrote – *It was the best of times. It became the worst. Robert Kennedy had won the California primary and it had meant so very much to him. He did not want to go downstairs to thank his supporters and deliver a victory statement until he was sure that he had the votes and that victory was really his. So, he walked down the hall on the Fifth floor of the Ambassador Hotel and he stopped to talk to someone and then he entered a room – Room 521 – and watched television to get the latest reports on the unbelievably slow Los Angeles returns. He saw Eugene McCarthy appear and tell his crowd that "We have not yet begun to fight." And he said, "John Paul Jones and the Bonhomme Richard. I guess I'm the Serapis." And then he walked to another room and his wife Ethel was there and brother-in-law Steve Smith and aides Fred Dutton and Dick Tuck and Dun Gifford and everyone was smiling and Ethel was bouncing a bit on the bed out of sheer happiness and it was the best of times. So, he went down the stairs to the Embassy Room and he thanked the people and kidded an old enemy – Mayor Sam Yorty – and he started to leave and suddenly, from an act of unreasoning hatred it was the worst of times. Robert Kennedy had known that it could end like this. He'd lived with the possibility – I think he even thought it a probability – for almost five years. Five years since his brother was struck down in Dallas. But he didn't let it show often and, when he did, it was with a touch of humor. Campaigning in Indiana, we were rolling down the runway about to take off for yet another stop and another crowd and another speech when suddenly the pilot cut the engines and stopped the take-off. Some minor adjustments were made and we started again and Kennedy turned and said, "I don't want to seem immodest but, if we don't make it, you fellas are going to be in small print."*

*And so, now, it is the worst of times – worse than you ever thought it would be – and you try to remember the better times to ease the pain of these times. There's the day the new senator from New York was walking down the hall to a committee meeting when a man in a loud tie came up and said, 'Ain't you one of them Kennedys? "Yes", he replied. And the man said, "Alright, which one are you?" And he replied, "I'm Bob." And the man said, "Uh huh. I thought so", and spun on his heel and walked away and the young senator shook his head and looked at you and you both smiled and shook your heads and now you think there aren't so many of "the Kennedys" anymore.*

*There are other little things that flash like instant pictures through your mind. The time earlier this week when you gave him a button you'd bought on Fisherman's Wharf in San Francisco that said, "Expand the White House. Here come the Kennedys" and the way he laughed when he read it and took it off to show to Ethel because she would laugh, too. Then, there was his concern for people, especially for children and for those who needed someone to stand up for them. He liked especially to talk with children. He had a special affinity for them and they for him. One afternoon, in the middle of a motorcade, he stopped and lay on the trunk of the car and gathered the children in the crowd around him and just talked about pets and what they wanted to be when they grew up. He always asked how many brothers and sisters they had and was always pleased when they said they had several. What he really wanted, I think, was to make the world better, to make life better for the children. There were those who called him ruthless. He wasn't. He was a totally compassionate man who cared very deeply and the depth of his concern would make him fight hard for what was right. It was not, for him, a question of personal gain but of what could be done.*

*His favorite quotation on the campaign – one which signaled the end of a speech – was by George Bernard Shaw. It read, "Some men see things as they are and ask why. I dream things that never were and ask why not."*

*In this worst of times, it is easy to ask why, but Robert Kennedy would still have been seeking that newer world and asking "why not."*

To be honest, the funeral at St. Patrick's Cathedral remains largely a blur. The famous church was crowded with political and show business celebrities as well as Kennedy family members. Eugene McCarthy was there. And Lyndon Johnson. Ted Kennedy – who truly was shattered by the loss of his brother – delivered the eulogy. His closing words stay with me still.

*My brother need not be idealized, or enlarged in death beyond what he was in life, to be remembered simply as a good and decent man, who saw wrong and tried to right it, saw suffering and tried to heal it, saw war and tried to stop it. Those of us who loved him and who take him to his rest today pray that what he was to us and what he wished for others will some day pass for all the world.*

Then, Ted Kennedy and Bob's son Joe, who remains a friend over all these years, led the procession out to Fifth Avenue and the waiting motorcade. Thirty buses would carry some 700 people to Grand Central Station where a special train was waiting to carry the casket, the family and so many people back to Washington for the burial in Arlington National Cemetery. The logistics alone were staggering. And the crowds who lined the streets mostly were silent in their display of grief. Half an hour behind schedule, the 21-car train pulled out of the station for the 226-mile trip to Washington. At the first station in Newark, New Jersey, some 7000-people lined the tracks, many holding small flags and with tears in their eyes. The scene was to be repeated at each station along the way. Those of us inside were glued to the windows when tragedy struck again. At Elizabeth station, a train en route to New York passed the funeral train and struck two of the trackside mourners, killing both. It was decided that Ethel Kennedy would not be told. But Kennedy advance man Jerry Bruno – himself something of a legend in political circles—confronted railroad officials and demand that security be improved or else the train would be halted right there on the tracks. The railroad officials surrendered to his demands. And the crowds continued all along the route. The nation and we journalists never had seen anything like it. And we probably never will again. As the train rolled slowly on, young Joe Kennedy – all of 15 years old – walked the entire length of the train greeting every passenger with the words, "Hello. I'm Joe Kennedy. Thank you for coming." Joe went on to become a member of Congress and founder of Citizens Energy in Boston. A short time later, Ethel Kennedy also walked the length of the train, greeting each person individually. It took 8-hours and 21-minutes for the train to reach Washington.

A motorcade was waiting at Union Station and most of the VIPs were herded on to buses and taken to Arlington National Cemetery. But there was a separate motorcade – the last of the campaign – for a handful of dignitaries, including the president and the press corps. We had our own bus, just as we did in the campaign. As had been the case everywhere, crowds lined the streets as the motorcade rolled along. The unwritten rule was that the press bus always followed next to the candidate. Our bus was 23rd in line. That was unacceptable. Frank Mankiewicz ordered the driver to swing out of line and pull in behind the family. This meant that President Johnson and Vice

President Humphrey had to follow behind the press bus. Their Secret Service agents were seriously not happy. An agent ordered the bus to get out of the line but the irrepressible Dick Tuck blew a whistle and the bus continued on. Then, the limousines tried pulling around the bus but press aide Dick Drayne leaped out and literally stood in front of the limousines, forcing them to stop. The first limo that he blocked was carrying the President. The Secret Service guys leaped forward and Drayne, with a huge grin on his face, got back on our bus. We applauded. It may have seemed unseemly to some but I am sure the family understood.

At the cemetery, I walked up the hill with longtime Kennedy friend and former Postmaster General Laurence O'Brien. The two of us were friends and remained so until his death at much too early an age. The family was gathered at the site next to the casket. Ethel and Ted said their final farewells and moved off. Other family members then moved forward. The press corps stayed until the very end. It is what you do.

Throughout much of the campaign, RFK was accompanied by his faithful dog Freckles – a Springer Spaniel—seen here waiting for his human pal who would not be returning.

# CHAPTER 11

Over the next several months, there were occasional gatherings of people who worked on RFK's presidential campaign and the reporters who covered it. Most of those took place at the Kennedy home at Hickory Hill. One of the most poignant took place in a darkened room at a Washington, D.C. hotel where photographers Stan Tretick of Look Magazine and Bill Eppridge of Life Magazine – two of the finest photo journalists of their time and both of whom had covered Robert Kennedy's campaign – put on a private showing of their campaign images. At the end, the room was filled not with applause, initially, but with absolute, respectful silence. Later, journalist Jules Witcover – my longtime friend – was to write in his book *85 Days – The Last Campaign of Robert Kennedy* – "*But for those to whom he was much more than his brother's brother, for those for whom he was the most electric personality of his time and place, Robert Francis Kennedy will be remembered not merely as one of a family triumvirate, but as one man who in his own moment in history moved people, and was moved by them, to a condition of hope in a time of national disillusionment.*"

Later that year, I came up with the idea of establishing a journalism award in RFK's memory. During a lengthy meeting with Kennedy counsellor (and my attorney) Fred Dutton, we put together an outline that we thought would be acceptable to Ted Kennedy. Then, we marched off to see him. It is fair to say that Ted was not wildly enthusiastic. He frankly doubted that a group of journalists could raise the money needed for such a program and draw the attention that would be necessary. However, he did somewhat skeptically give me the green light to proceed.

Ted was right, of course, when he said that we would need to raise money. However, he was wrong about whether we could pull it off. Dick Harwood of the Washington Post went to his senior management to get them to contribute. So did John Herbers of the New York Times and John Lindsey of Newsweek and Warren Rogers of Life Magazine and Bob Clark of ABC News. I called Bill Small at CBS who not only arranged for a large contribution but made his screening room available for viewing video entries for the award. For the hard work of these and others, I remain eternally grateful. Then, with the award initially funded, we all trouped to Hickory Hill to serenade Ethel with Christmas carols and present her with a copy of the award which was established in the name of Bob and Ethel's newly born daughter – Rory Elizabeth Katherine Kennedy *"in the hope of helping, in a small way, to shape the newer world her father sought."* Now, some 50 years later, the program – the Robert F. Kennedy Journalism Awards – remains one of the most respected and popular journalism awards program in the country – second only to the Pulitzer prizes – and the only such award named after a major political figure. Not bad for a bunch of hard bitten journalists. Baby Rory Kennedy has gone on to become a highly regarded producer of documentaries and lives in the Los Angeles area with her husband and three children.

Meanwhile, the 1968 presidential campaign continued on its way to the Democratic nomination in Chicago. Eugene McCarthy remained in the race but it became increasingly clear that Vice President Hubert Humphrey now would be the nominee. I went off to travel for a while with New York Governor Nelson Rockefeller who was challenging former Vice President Richard Nixon for the Republican nomination. Rockefeller was very wealthy and his campaign was a bit unusual to say the least. Rockefeller was smart, articulate, had a big, warm grin and a desire to shake every hand in sight – sometimes more than once. The odds were stacked against him. The liberal governor of New York was not likely to win over the GOP faithful. However, traveling with his campaign made a decent transition back into the presidential coverage. Because this was Rockefeller, his campaign plane tended toward the extravagant. There were times that we were served pheasant and champagne for dinner. And the plane seats really were comfortable. It was a nice diversion but clouds were gathering over Chicago where the Democrats were to hold their nominating convention.

Had Robert Kennedy lived, the Chicago convention might have been fairly routine. Mayor Richard Daley was a longtime Kennedy family ally and his support for RFK was assured. But, now, the convention was en route to becoming a brawl with Mayor Daley supporting Vice President Humphrey over Eugene McCarthy whom Daley disliked. In addition, anti-Vietnam War demonstrators were pouring into the city and most of them supported McCarthy. As fate would have it, my hotel room at the convention overlooked Lincoln Park where most of the clashes occurred between demonstrators and police. Both Sen. McCarthy and Sen. George McGovern of South Dakota came to my room for a better view of what was happening in the street below. McGovern – a thoroughly decent man – had agreed to be a stand-in for the Kennedy supporters so that they would have someone for whom to cast their votes other than Humphrey and McCarthy. McCarthy seemed to view the rioting as something of a distraction. McGovern clearly was upset by what he saw, shaking his head in what appeared to be sincere sadness. Much has been written about what took place in the streets during the convention and the clashes subsequently were termed a "police riot" by a special investigating panel. One of my most vivid memories was down on the street seeing several police officers literally hurl a young woman through the plate glass window of the hotel restaurant. Amazingly, she was not seriously injured.

# CHAPTER 12

Then, it was off to Miami for the Republican convention where the nomination of Richard Nixon was assured. The only real question mark was over who he might pick for his running mate. One of the possible candidates was Maryland governor Spiro T. (Ted) Agnew. On the flight from Washington to Miami, I would up seated next to Agnew's wife Judy – an unpretentious, soft-spoken woman who was deathly afraid of flying. So, I wound up holding her hand and chatting with her during the flight. A couple of days later, I saw her standing in front of the hotel in which the Agnews were staying. I paused to say "hello" and noticed a perplexed expression on her face. I asked her what was going on and she told me that Secret Service agents had arrived a short time ago and were moving the couple's belongings into another hotel – the one in which the Nixon's were staying and she did not know why. But I understood instantly. Agnew was Nixon's choice for Vice President. I raced to the nearest telephone – no cell phones in those days – and called the Metromedia News desk in New York with the story. We beat all of the competition by a mile. My relationship with the Agnews remained friendly even after he had unnecessarily made enemies of most of the political press corps. Eventually, Agnew was forced to resign the Vice Presidency because of corruption. However, he had a couple more roles to play in my career.

When Agnew headed out on his own to campaign, I was tapped to tag along. One of the stops was in Las Vegas where some of my colleagues decided to indulge in all that Sin City had to offer. Several did not return to the campaign plane until shortly before takeoff.

Among them was veteran Baltimore Sun reporter Gene Oishi who was of Japanese descent and had covered Agnew when the candidate was governor of Maryland. When Agnew got back on the plane, he noticed a truly wasted Oishi asleep in his seat. Agnew immediately asked, "What's the matter with the fat jap?" Several reporters – unfamiliar with the lengthy relationship between Agnew and Oishi – wrote stories suggesting that Agnew was racially insensitive. Overall, he may have been but, in this case, I felt his comment had been taken out of context and I said so.

Most veteran political journalists now expected Richard Nixon would be the next president of the United States. The Nixon campaign had billboards that declared "Nixon's The One" and featured an open briefcase in which he was supposed to have a plan to end the war in Vietnam. However, he never spelled out the details. Nixon definitely had a dark side as became more evident after his election when he authorized illegal steps that lead to the Watergate investigation and his eventual resignation from the presidency. I first experienced Nixon's dark side during the 1968 presidential campaign. As a general rule, a candidate for president has at least one member of the traveling press corps with him at all times. Basically, it is a body watch in case something bad happens. During a stop in Florida, I happened to be the designated close by reporter usually known as the pool reporter. That reporter's job is to report back to everyone else in the press corps should anything untoward happen. Nixon and his wife Pat were shaking hands while working their way through a crowd of supporters. Accompanied by his Secret Service detail and myself, Nixon arrived first at the waiting elevator that was to take the couple up to their hotel room. He wanted to go up right away but one of the agents reminded him that Mrs. Nixon was still shaking hands a few feet away. Nixon responded, "Fuck her. Take me up." That insight into Nixon's character never left me. Nor did I report that incident because, in those days, it took something a lot more dramatic to really become news.

Then there was a very different moment with some of the Nixon senior staff. For the most part, these were likeable guys and we occasionally had drinks together. One evening, after a campaign stop in Cincinnati, Ohio, someone suggested that we all go across the border into Covington, Kentucky, on the other side of the Ohio River. Allegedly, there was a hot nightclub near the river that featured dancing girls and whatever. So, the Nixon senior staff corralled a handful of us from the traveling press corps and off we went. Little did we dream what awaited us on the other side of the river. We barely had taken our seats at a table when a man in the front row leaped up on stage and tried to grab one of the dancing girls. She kicked him in the head and a brawl broke out. Painfully aware that this would be bad publicity for all of us, we ducked under the tables and crawled rapidly to the front door and dashed outside, flagged down a couple of cabs and scurried back to Ohio. Never since then have I ever heard a single mention of that seedy memory from the campaign. And Nixon went on to win the 1968 election.

There is one more Nixon story – one that truly surprised me. After he was ensconced in the White House, Nixon and his senior staff – Robert Haldeman and John Ehrlichman – began preparing what soon became known as the White House enemies list. Not surprisingly, a number of journalists made that list and it was considered a minor badge of integrity. My friend John Sears – a senior Nixon political advisor with whom I had an annual wager on the outcome of each fall's Purdue-Notre Dame football game – informed me one day that I had not made the enemies list. I was dismayed and surprised and asked him why. He told me that both Haldeman and Erhlichman had urged Nixon to put my name on the list but that the President responded, "No. He is a son-of-a-bitch, but he is a fair son-of-a-bitch." I guess that falls under the heading of being damned with faint praise.

# CHAPTER 13

1969 also included yet another tragedy for the Kennedy family. I was having dinner at an Italian restaurant with my attorney – Fred Dutton. Fred had been a policy advisor and political consultant to both John and Robert Kennedy and was one of the smartest and most decent men in politics that I ever met. Our main course had yet to arrive on that July evening when Fred was summoned to take a telephone call. He returned to the table looking dismayed and asked if I would be interested in flying with him to Hyannis, Massachusetts. "Why", I asked, "would I want to do that at this late hour?" Fred replied, "Because Ted Kennedy has just driven off a bridge with Mary Jo Kopechne and I have booked the last two seats on the last flight out of National Airport to Boston." Without another word, I stood up and we raced for the door and hopped into my car. We just barely made the flight. When we landed in Boston, I rented a car while Fred grabbed a pay phone and was brought up to date. Ted was shaken but mostly OK. However, Mary Jo drowned. The news hit both of us hard as we knew Mary Jo to be a hard-working and dedicated member of Robert Kennedy's staff. She had been attending a reunion on Chappaquiddick Island of the six young women known as the "Boiler Room Girls" who had worked very hard in a windowless room for Robert Kennedy's presidential campaign. Ted Kennedy was hosting the gathering and offered to give Mary Jo a ride so that she could catch the last ferry to Edgartown where she was staying. However, he made a wrong turn and his car plunged off a narrow bridge and overturned in the water.

For several hours, I had the story mostly to myself. However, by the next morning, a small army of reporters had arrived. I remained there for several days, talking a couple of times privately with Ethel Kennedy who was at the family home near Hyannisport, as well as with family consigliere Steve Smith, who was married to Jean Kennedy, and with Ted Sorenson who had arrived to help craft the speech that Sen. Kennedy was to deliver to the nation telling his version of what happened.

One evening, while my pal Hayes Gorey of Time Magazine and I were having a drink at the hotel's small piano bar, we were joined by Kennedy press secretary Dick Drayne. Dick was very popular with the entire press corps and known for his wicked and irreverent sense of humor. During a pause in the conversation, Dick looked over at the piano player and said to us, "I guess this would not be a good time to request that he play '*Bridge Over Troubled Water*.'" The song by Paul Simon and Art Garfunkle was a big hit at the time. Hayes and I were both reduced to a major case of the giggles. Ted delivered his speech explaining what had happened and I returned home to Washington. Several months later, Ted sat down with me in the Metromedia television studios and gave his first on-the-record televised interview about what had happened that tragic evening and his plans for the future. At that point, a bid for the presidency was barely considered.

Throughout 1969, I had been serving as Washington Bureau Chief of the Metromedia News network. During that time, a young college graduate had started working at our local affiliate WTTG. We needed someone to cover weekends for the network and I had seen how she handled the news at WTTG. So, I offered her the job as weekend reporter for the network. Her name was – and still is – Connie Chung. She became one of the smartest and hardest working women in television news. We remained friends with both of us following different paths that took us to Los Angeles. Occasionally, she and her then boyfriend and subsequently husband – Maury Povich – would meet at my house before going out on dates so that people at KCBS-TV would not know they were dating.

With the arrival of the 1970, I longed to return to full time reporting and analysis plus hosting our very successful weekend television interview series. After some negotiating, I was given the new title of Chief National & Political Correspondent and Al Christian moved into my former office as Bureau Chief. Our team was considered among the best of the news organizations in Washington and we worked very hard to live up to that assessment. But 1970 was to become a year of transition.

We had developed our weekly interview program *Profile* into being competitive with the big guys – ABC, CBS and NBC. Increasingly, quotes from our program began appearing in news reports on Monday morning. In addition to the highly watched interview with Ted Kennedy after the Chappaquiddic accident, we scored the first interview with then Vice President Spiro Agnew following his "nattering nabobs of negativism" attack on journalists covering the Nixon Administration. We played host to a number of high profile guests on the program week in and week out. Many of those guests appeared because of my personal relationship with them and/ or their press secretaries or both. Similarly, at the annual high profile Congressional Correspondents and White House Correspondents dinners, we frequently had the table with the best political guests. All of that was solid testimony to the influence and the respect that we had developed in the nation's capital.

In 1970, Sargent Shriver – the husband of Kennedy sister Eunice Shriver – returned from his post as Ambassador to France and began considering a run for governor of Maryland. Some of the family members who had not appreciated his taking the ambassador's post in the Johnson Administration – were less than enthusiastic. One evening, Ethel Kennedy invited a group of us that included John Glenn, Hays Gorey from Time Magazine, Eunice Shriver, Fred Dutton and a handful of others including myself to dinner at Hickory Hill. After the dinner, Ethel – with her usual directness – announced that she was taking a poll on whether Shriver should run for governor. Everyone in the room, except Eunice, voted against Sarge running. Eunice was not happy and left immediately. It took her a while to forgive most of us for that vote of no confidence in her husband.

In the early 70s, antiwar protests were being organized by a group - the Vietnam Moratorium – headed by Sam Brown and David Mixner and David Hawk. Hawk died much earlier than he should have. However Brown and Mixner continued to campaign on issues they cared strongly about. In the early Seventies, they took to referring to me as the only establishment reporter they could trust. That trust allowed me to listen in on a series of meetings that helped me better understand the dynamics of what they were doing.

Meanwhile, storm clouds were gathering at Metromedia that we did not see or anticipate. On a Friday in the spring of 1970, I arrived at the office to discover a scene of disarray and dismay. John Kluge – the owner of Metromedia Broadcasting – had decided he no longer could afford the cost of the prestigious Washington Bureau. Even though it was morning, Al Christian was sitting in his office with an open bottle of Jim Beam and a stack of pink slips. Simply put – the bureau was history and all of us were out of jobs. It was a reminder that no matter how well you do your job and how much acclaim you receive, in the end, it really is all about the money.

# CHAPTER 14

For me, the end of the Metromedia Washington Bureau brought an entirely new and different set of circumstances. Joe Blatchford – previously a member of Congress from California and a professional tennis player who made it all the way to the British championship tournament of Wimbledon – was appointed director of the Peace Corps. Joe was a good guy with a sense of humor and a willingness to stand up for what he thought was right. It turned out that he also was good friends with Frank Mankiewicz, who gave Joe a call and recommended me for a senior Peace Corps position. I accepted a job as Deputy Director of Public Affairs for the Peace Corps. Also in the office were two relatively liberal Republican advertising experts – Jack Porter and Bill Novelli. Working with them was a pleasure. The first thing I did was hire Loudell Insley out of Ted Kennedy's office and make her pretty much the office manager and confidant. We did walk something of a thin line because the Nixon White House would have found some of our activities and personal histories difficult to swallow. And eventually they did.

Working at the Peace Corps was a very special experience. There were so many really good people working there who were dedicated to the founding principles of the agency. Early on, a decision was made to improve relations with some of the countries in West Africa where Peace Corps volunteers were working. The fact that I spoke French – the common language of the region – resulted in my name being put on the list to go to Africa and spend some time there. Our somewhat fluid itinerary included Liberia, Niger, Upper Volta (now known as Burkina Faso), the Ivory Coast and Dahomey (now known as the Republic of Benin). In each and every country, the volunteers with whom I met were exceptional people devoted to improving the lives of the people in the countries to which they had been assigned. Of course, the trip produced a number of stories which I will attempt to recount.

The graphic mark combined with our agency name
creates the official Peace Corps logo.

We were warned to be especially alert for black and green mambas – a very deadly African snake. We were given anti-venom but cautioned that we had only 60 seconds between being bitten and injecting ourselves. After that, it would be too late. After arriving in Niamey – the capital of Niger, some volunteers told us the story – absolutely true – of a female volunteer recently bitten by a mamba. She was given up for lost with shallow breathing and fading fast when the village witchdoctor arrived. He wrapped the site of the bite with leaves and then killed a chicken and wrapped the chicken's body around the leg at the bite site. Then, for 48 hours, he chanted and prayed over the young volunteer. At the end of the second day, she regained consciousness and went on to make a full recovery. The story was verified by several people.

The Niger River flows just outside of Niamey. One morning, I rose early and went for a walk along the river. It was a lovely early morning before the heat of the day set in. As I walked around a corner, I came pretty much face to face with a lion. Fortunately, it was a male lion and both of us turned tail and headed in opposite directions. On another day, in downtown Niamey, people started shouting that someone was coming. Then, literally out of a cloud of dust appeared a group of Tuareg warriors. They were dressed in flowing blue robes and riding on white horses. Long swords swung from their waists. They were a totally amazing sight. However, women were busy getting their children off the street. In those days, the Tuaregs were known as kidnappers and slave traders and not to be messed with. Legend has it that the Tuaregs were descendants of the famed British lost legion in the desert. Certainly, they were much lighter skinned that anyone else native to the area and always disappeared back into the desert. They stayed in town for two days – mostly doing some bartering. I spent some of that time doing some bartering, too. For $20.00 US, I came away with a hand-made Tuareg dagger which I have kept safely to this very day. That afternoon, the Tuareg warriors mounted their horses and, with a flourish of their blue robes, they disappeared in a cloud of dust back into the desert.

We also spent some time in Dahomey where people usually seemed to assume that a white person had to be from France and, thus, very unpopular. Fortunately, when they learned we were from les Etats Unis, they became much more friendly. Dahomey was known as the home of the python cult which was headquartered in an abandoned French fort in the jungle known as Wydah – sometimes spelled Ouida. It has roughly 50 pythons living there. So, I decided to trek with some other Peace Corps folks out to the python temple. The old French cannons stared down at us from the walls of the fort. We had to allow a pair of pythons to wrap themselves around our arms as a test to see whether we should be allowed in. Fortunately, all of us passed the test. Later, I learned that the pythons were fairly friendly, used to visitors and fed regularly. No threat to anyone. Even so, I thought it was a pretty cool experience.

One evening, I visited a rather remote village to meet with the chief and smooth over some ruffled feathers. For a while, we sat around drinking palm wine from mismatched 8oz tumblers. Palm wine is a lot stronger than our domestic wine. Then, we were served bowls of jungle rat stew. It is important to note that jungle rats are not plagued with vermin like city rats. So, the stew was pretty good. Then, the chief said he had something important to say. He wanted me to meet his 11-year-old daughter. She looked pretty much like any other 11-year-old except that her teeth had been filed to very sharp points that were quite visible when she smiled. The chief wanted me to marry his daughter and take her back to America with me. Now, I had had a couple of glasses of strong palm wine but not THAT many glasses. I explained that I was already married to two wives with many children and our religion did not allow me to have another wife and that I would be punished severely if I were to bring home a third wife. He finally dropped the idea and we left shortly thereafter. Apparently he did not bear a grudge and the Peace Corps volunteers were allowed to remain.

A few days later, I returned to Washington, D.C., and more adventures in the world of the Peace Corps. Some people, including President Nixon's top advisors, were trying to get rid of the Peace Corps. Robert Haldeman – one of those called by outsiders "the Germans" – was among those pushing to have the agency shut down. However, Joe Blatchford was no shrinking violet. During one Oval Office meeting, Blatchford stood up at the end and appeared to be deferring to Haldeman by holding the door open for him. Haldeman arrogantly stepped through the door, at which point Joe shut the door, turned around and told President Nixon he had some things to say without being interrupted by Haldeman. Nonetheless, White House efforts continued and Budget Director George Schultz and Vice President Agnew were to appear on Capitol Hill to testify against the Peace Corps funding during the same week that the Peace Corps celebrated its 10th anniversary. We had been organizing an anniversary party when we got wind of the planned testimony. Members of the Kennedy family – including Ethel Kennedy and Eunice Shiver – were scheduled to attend. I called my old friend Charlie McWhorter – a long time Nixon insider with definite White House clout and a fan of the Peace Corps – and ask if he could get Agnew and Schultz to do a drop by at the party. Charlie said that he could and would give us a heads up when they were on the way. We immediately sharply increased our outreach to the networks, the

Washington Post, and every other news outlet in DC, promising some dramatic news would take place at the party. Charlie delivered on his promised heads up and, when Agnew and Schultz stepped off the elevator, they were greeted by Ethel and Eunice and other family members and a small army of cameras and reporters. The photos, video and print stories were everywhere. The Congressional appearances by Agnew and Schultz were cancelled. The strategy was a total success but I knew that my days at the Peace Corps headquarters were numbered. Fortunately, at about that time, CBS made me an offer I could not refuse.

# CHAPTER 15

Bill Small, the CBS News Washington Bureau Chief, recommended that I join the CBS News operations on the West Coast where I would work out of the KNX facilities in Los Angeles as both a network and local reporter. The news director was an egotistical man named Jim Zaillian. He was fond of boasting that his newsroom was his personal United Nations because he had people of every color working there. Skill. Experience. None of that mattered. You just needed to fit his quota. On the other hand, the general manager was George Nicholaw and he was outstanding.

As it would happen, we were in yet another presidential election year. Sen. George McGovern was slightly favored to win the Democratic Party nomination but equally assured, it seemed, of losing the general election. I genuinely liked McGovern – a soft spoken World War II veteran and, indeed, a genuine war hero who cared deeply about some of the issues that had been important to Robert Kennedy. He opposed the war in Vietnam, cared about hunger in America and was a thoroughly decent man. Among the many elected officials I have known, George and his wife Eleanor rank near the top. CBS sent me to Miami to cover the Democratic convention. It was a political disaster for the Democrats. After a series of delays, McGovern's acceptance speech finally was scheduled for the wee hours of the morning and heard or seen by a relatively small group of people. Some of us whiled away the time by talking long walks on a nearby golf course. I was joined by actresses Candice Bergan and Marlo Thomas and the three of us discussed subjects large and small and still had time left to return to the convention hall for McGovern's speech. I wished George well but a Nixon landslide was in the making and the man from South Dakota carried only two states, including losing his home state.

During much of this time, I was spending spare moments on the tennis court. I took lessons from Wimbledon champion Darlene Hard and tennis pro Barky Boodakian. My frequent partner was Jonathan Peck – son of actor Gregory Peck. We played at tennis courts located near the Greek Theater in Griffith Park. The setting is awesome and relatively peaceful. Often coyotes and deer wander past. The courts do not have lights for night games. One evening, as I left the courts, I turned on the car headlights and they illuminated a mountain lion in the middle of the road eyeing a cluster of deer on the adjoining golf course. The big cat gave me an evil look and moved away. When I got home, I called the park ranger office to report what I had seen and the ranger who answered replied that they were aware of the mountain lion in the park and that there also was a second one, too, but they did not talk about it much to avoid scaring people. These days, people take pride in the presence of P22 –a mountain lion who figured out how to sneak into the Los Angeles Zoo, eat a Koala bear and leave without being seen

Meanwhile, politics took a back seat to crime less than two years later when a radical Bay Area group called the Symbionese Liberation Army (SLA) kidnapped Patricia Hearst – the 19-year-old grand-daughter of newspaper magnate William Randolph Hearst. Miss Hearst enthusiastically joined the SLA a few months later and participated in a bank robbery while also posing as a gun-toting model for an SLA poster. She later would claim she had been brain washed. On May 17, 1974, Los Angeles police received a tip that the SLA members were hiding out at a house in South Central Los Angeles and some 400 officers were dispatched to the address. They were followed by most of the Los Angeles press corps. On a gamble, I worked my way around to the back of the house and met an LAPD Lieutenant who also was in the rear alley. It seemed as though we were the only ones there when suddenly an enormous gunfight erupted. People inside the house and police outside were blasting away at each other. The lieutenant and I kept our heads down and were watching as the house burst into flames triggered by tear gas and smoke grenades. Bullets often flew over our heads. All of that time, I was on the air live on KNX and across the nation via CBS. The battle lasted for about two hours and six of the SLA members died inside including their leader Donald DeFreese, who committed suicide. Later I received several awards for my reporting at the scene.

I was not quite done with the SLA. The group's new leaders – William and Emily Harris – were placed on trial in Los Angeles and I was sent to cover at least part of the trial. Their attorney was widely respected defense attorney Leonard Weinglass who also had represented the Chicago 7 defendants after the rioting at the 1968 Democratic convention. Over the years, Lennie and I had become friendly and I tried never to miss one of his appearances in court because he was absolutely a master of the courtroom and watching him at work was a pleasure. This trial was no different. Lennie was a prime exponent of the theory that no matter what the result of a trial is in the courtroom the actual result is produced outside the court-room when attorneys talk to reporters. As a result, he made himself readily available to reporters after each court session.

A couple of years later, we both were back in court again when Lennie took on the case of two Native Americans – Paul Skyhorse and Richard Mohawk – who were accused of the murder of a Los Angeles cab driver. They were acquitted following a lengthy trial after what only can be described as a brilliant defense by Lennie and his legal team that included turning the tables on the government's case and getting one of the prosecution witnesses to admit in court that he was the actual killer of the cab driver. I often have said that Lennie should have charged admission for people to watch him in court and I was very lucky to have been paid to be there.

By then, I had left CBS and moved on to where I really wanted to be – NBC News. I was in the Burbank Bureau – one of NBC's best operations – and delighted to be there. Because of my polit-ical experience, I often bounced back to Washington, D.C., for some stories. I also continued to chair an influential group of polit-ical reporters called the Friday Group because, initially, we always met on Fridays. The group was patterned after the well-known

Christian Science Monitor breakfasts held by political reporters in Washington, D.C. Most of the members were print reporters, although we expanded to add television reporters as well. However, no cameras were in the breakfast room at a hotel. The cameras stayed outside for post-breakfast interviews. Our guests included presidential candidates, California candidates for governor, elected officials, senior government officers and more. We often were described as an influential group. In a sense, we were. Politicians and their consultants wanted a forum from which they could reach the vote rich Los Angeles area. They also wanted to establish some sort of working relationship with the region's political reporters. In those days, there were quite a few regional political reporters and most were very good. One paper – the Los Angeles Times – was very territorial. If you worked for their Washington Bureau – as my friend Jules Witcover, a highly regarded political columnist did – then you had to stop reporting once you crossed the California state line. At that point, Times political reporter Richard Bergholz, who was based in Los Angeles, took over. It drove Witcover and others who were traveling with presidential campaigns absolutely nuts. I often was asked who my favorite guests were at the breakfasts. I always found every guest interesting. But I did have a list of those whose candor always was refreshing. They included GOP political campaign consultant Stuart Spencer, Governor Pete Wilson, Governor Jerry Brown, Sen. Dianne Feinstein, Ronald Reagan, Sen. Alan Cranston, Los Angeles Mayor Tom Bradley and Democratic Party leader Charles T. Manatt. We even had a few rare moments. The Friday Group lasted for well over a decade and was worth the effort it took to create it and to attract good guests. Los Angeles Times reporter Richard Bergholz was a founding member of the group. As his retirement day approached, we arranged for the group to gather along with some political consultants. About 15 minutes into the breakfast, a strategically located telephone rang. On the other end of the speaker phone was President Reagan calling from the White House to wish Dick well in retirement. It was a classic Reagan political roast routine and we all loved it—especially Dick who often had clashed with Reagan over the years.

From the mid-Seventies through the Eighties and beyond, I covered politics, environmental stories and the space program, along with a big earthquake and a few other developments. It was during this time that I married Mariko Fukuda – a television producer – and we had two great children – son Dylan and daughter Courtney. However, the marriage did not last. My interest in all these stories, however, continued unabated. All of these stories genuinely interested me and some were totally fascinating. I will come back to the politics later but, first, the space program.

Jet Propulsion Laboratory La Canada Flintridge California

# CHAPTER 16

Two of the major centers of space flight activity were in Southern California – Edwards Air Force Base in the Mojave Desert and the famed Jet Propulsion Laboratory (JPL) on the north edge of Pasadena. JPL was home to an amazing group of brilliant scientists – mostly affiliated with Cal Tech University. The facility itself is funded by the federal government through NASA and managed by the California Institute of Technology. It was there – while covering a multitude of stories – that my college background in chemistry finally paid off. During the two Viking landing on Mars and some other robotic encounters, the results involved organometallic compounds and that was in my scientific wheelhouse. In fact, that knowledge gave me an edge on many of the reporters covering events at JPL and afforded me the opportunity to develop relationships with some of the brightest scientists in the world. I spent hours sitting on chairs on the JPL campus talking with the widely renowned scientists including Carl Sagan – co-creator of the popular television series Cosmos. Some of my favorite conversations were with Carl, his wife Ann Druyan and Cosmos co-creator Gentry Lee who remains a friend and one of the most brilliant people I ever have met. Also in that category are Ed Stone and Bruce Murray, both of whom served as JPL directors during most of the years that I covered developments at JPL. Later, I also establish an ongoing friendship with Carolyn Porco – an outstanding planetary scientist who rose to prominence during the Voyager program because of her ability to explain such items as Saturn's many rings in terms a television viewer easily could understand. Carolyn went on to become Imaging Director of the Cassini mission – which she described as like driving a Lamborghini – to Saturn and a recipient of the prestigious Carl Sagan award at a packed ceremony at which I was honored to have been asked to introduce her. Carolyn moved on to a prestigious position as Distinguished Scholar in the Astronomy Department at UC Berkeley.

Covering science subjects for broadcast news can be challenging and sometimes just goofy. During the landing of Viking 1 on Mars, I received a phone call at home in the middle of the night telling me to rush to JPL because the lander had sent back a photo of a rock with carving on it. Well, I thought, it probably says Welcome to Mars. Nonetheless, I raced out to JPL and took one look at the rock and basically declared "you have to be kidding me!" Yes. It was a rock. Yes, it had some pock marked features but the only carving was done by wind erosion. It later turned out that someone working at the Associated Press had seen the image, misinterpreted it and put it out on the wire service. Several hours were spent debunking the story.

There also were some very good moments. There was the night that guitarist, singer, songwriter Chuck Berry serenaded the NASA scientists and their staff on a warm summer evening at JPL. He tore the place up and had aliens been looking down they would have seen the heat signature rise. From time to time, science fiction writers would stop by. I got to meet and chat with such amazing people as Ray Bradbury, Theodore Sturgeon, Robert Heinlein and Poul Anderson, among others. Of course, there also was the thrill of watching the first photos of Mars come down from Viking One and later Viking 2. There were the Voyagers with their enduring images of Neptune and Uranus and Saturn – the very real Lord of the Rings. More photos of Mars from Curiosity and Opportunity and Spirit. And Galileo at Jupiter. During my time at CNN, we had a semi-permanent broadcast center at JPL and our reporting became so dominant that other networks began sending their camera crews, producers and correspondents out to try to compete with us. By then, of course, we essentially owned JPL in terms of news coverage. There also were some other days. When the space shuttle Challenger exploded shortly after lift-off from Cape Canaveral in Florida, on January 28, 1986, killing all the astronauts aboard, I was at JPL. A day or two later, I found Gentry Lee in the darkened projection room running and re-running the video feed of the disaster. When I asked what he was doing, he replied that he was searching for the cause of the crash and told me that he was convinced the two O-rings that made the booster rocket and the main body of the shuttle separate had failed – probably due to having become too cold while waiting to be launched. He said I could use the information but could not attribute it to him – something that often happened with the scientists and engineers working at JPL. Gentry later was appointed to the special panel investigating the cause of the Challenger explosion and the panel confirmed Gentry's early analysis – the O-rings.

Some years later, my wife Gloria and I were in the audience at JPL when NASA awarded our friend actress June Lockhart the agency's prestigious Exceptional Public Achievement Award. June – who starred on so many television shows (including Lost in Space) and movies—became only the fourth person and the first woman to be so honored. Afterward, it was hugs all around with this longtime pal.

Meanwhile, the first series of space shuttle landings took place out at Edwards Air Force Base. The shuttles were assembled at Rockwell International's facility in Palmdale, California, not far from the landing site at Edwards. The assembled shuttle was hauled over back roads to the Air Force base and then put on the back of a specially designed and equipped Boeing 747 and flown to Cape Kennedy in Florida for launching. A working orbiter was built to test the aerodynamic design, but not to go into outer space. The initial orbiter was called the Enterprise after the "Star Trek" starship. The Enterprise flew numerous flight and landing tests, where it was launched from the Boeing 747 and glided to a landing at Edwards Air Force Base. I was present for those tests and spent a lot of time talking with various astronauts while watching the Enterprise come in for its test landings. NBC had me in the anchor chair to cover the test landings and the early spaceflights. The early lift offs and landings were dramatic moments of tension both for the shuttle managers and those of us who covered the events. The first night landing really was awesome as the shuttle appeared out of the night sky and coasted to a perfect landing amid the glowing lights at Edwards. By the time the two tragedies occurred with Columbia and Challenger, most of the flights had become routine along with the double sonic booms that heralded the arrival of the spacecraft over Southern California. After a while, we used NASA footage to cover the launches and landings. That is one reason why I was out at JPL when one of the two disasters occurred.

In 1989, a major earthquake severely shook San Francisco. ABC News and CNN promptly chartered a jet to get us to the Bay Area because the San Francisco Airport was closed. We landed at the Santa Cruz airport which was the closest available landing site. The runway was short and we barely were able to stop in time. As we got off the plane, NBC cameraman Bruce Gray, with whom I often had worked, approached and said to me "I thought for a minute there that you all were going to be crispy critters." I replied, "Me, too." Fortunately, all went well, and I wound up doing some good stories before moving up the coast to San Francisco. In fact, no less than the New York Times actually had a story praising my coverage. I have been looking ever since for a copy of that story. One of the major wineries in the Santa Cruz area suffered significant damage. The winery's wine expert said they had two options – either the quake had so shaken that year's vintage that it would be worthless or it would have triggered a really good reaction. Months later, the verdict was in and I enjoyed a bottle of their cabernet. Eventually, I reached San Francisco itself and longtime friend and colleague Tom Brokaw from NBC and I wound up standing next to each other doing our live shots from the severely damaged part of the City by the Bay.

One night, on my way back to my hotel in the darkened city, I heard a woman screaming. I looked to see what was going on and saw a man trying to steal the woman's purse. I yelled at him to stop and he turned toward me waving a knife. Fortunately, I was quicker and better trained than he was and the woman and I came out of it all in good shape. He was less fortunate.

# CHAPTER 17

Being in Los Angeles also revived my longstanding interest in music. I started hanging out at a popular Mexican restaurant – Lucy's El Adobe – and became close friends with the owners – Frank and Lucy Casado. They even hung my picture on their wall where it rested among many photos of the very best of actors, musicians and politicians, most notably California Governor Jerry Brown. I first went there with my longtime friend Tom Quinn who was Brown's chief political strategist. I wrote a lengthy magazine article about Lucy and Frank, their children James, Patty and Daryl and the restaurant and they liked it so much that they framed it and hung it on a restaurant wall.

Frank Casado was the dominant figure in the restaurant and his wife Lucy, after whom the restaurant was named, was the "mother" of many of the restaurant's guests. The members of the Eagles were among the many talented men who Lucy referred to as her "boys". Linda Ronstadt was an adopted member of the family. So many people from the entertainment industry dined there that you could fill a book with the stories they either told or were told about them. I once took actress Loretta Swit – one of the stars of the wildly successful TV series MASH – to the restaurant and triggered a series of rumors that we were a couple – stories that she and I both vigorously denied. When Frank Casado died, I was asked to be one of the pallbearers and Linda sang a stunning version of Ave Maria that echoed off the rafters of the church.

Jamming with T Bone Burnett

Over time, I became friends with Don Henley, co-founder of the Eagles, singer and song writer John David Souther, acclaimed musician and producer T Bone Burnett, who has remained a pal for many years, and Linda Ronstadt, among others. J.D was blessed with a strong personality and became the honorary uncle to my then young children Dylan and Courtney and later Dylan's godfather. When Eagles co-founder Glenn Frey died, a private memorial was held at the Los Angeles Forum and tears were mixed with laughter as various attendees regaled the audience of friends and family with numerous stories. Don and the Eagles generally were represented by music titan Irving Azoff – a hardnosed yet highly successful music industry manager for whom I always have had a very high regard. The Eagles media contact for years has been my friend Larry Solters. It is no overstatement to say that Larry may be the most respected media manager in the business. His word is as bankable among jour-nalists as a briefcase full of platinum. Another industry friend was Joe Smith – a former Boston deejay who became head of Elektra/Asylum records and then of Capitol Records. A great story teller, Joe's word always has been good.

Nicolette Larson

When Linda famously started dating then governor Jerry Brown, who I also knew, I wound up spending time with them and with Linda's singing pal Nicolette Larson. The three of us – Linda, Nicolette and I – would ride in Linda's Mercedes with the top down and sing a wide variety of songs while driving to Venice Beach to go roller skating. When Linda learned that I had skated professionally in college, she insisted that I coach her. Nic and I also took time off on our own. We remained friends until her untimely death from cerebral edema. On one occasion, Jerry was staying at Linda's beach house in Malibu, when I dropped by. The governor was working on a list of Superior Court judges who had been recommended for promotions. He asked my views of some of them and mostly I said each one was a good choice. Then he mentioned a judge whom I absolutely despised. I told Jerry the man had serious ethical issues and did not deserve to be promoted. I was pleased when Jerry picked up a pen and crossed that man's name off the list.

Jerry was planning a trip to Africa – a continent he never had visited—and he invited Linda to go with him. She called me and asked what I thought. And I gave the matter very serious thought because Linda is a serious person, an awesome human being and one of my all-time favorite people and she deserved a thoughtful answer. Eventually, I said that I thought she should go. However, I cautioned her to be prepared for an onslaught of media coverage. Little did either of us fully anticipate how big that onslaught would be. I don't think Linda was harmed by the attention, although she did not really enjoy it, but I am sure that Jerry probably benefited from it. As I mentioned, Linda has a serious and studious side. Once, when I asked her what she wanted for her birthday, she replied "a book". She is an omnivorous reader and I have been recommending books to her over the course of many years. My daughter Courtney was and is a big Linda Ronstadt fan. One day, when Linda was rehearsing with a Mariachi band – she sang in Spanish, too – I took Courtney with me to introduce her to my longtime friend. While we waited, we heard Linda and a trumpet player running up the scale together – vocal and trumpet notes in synch all the way to the top. Awesome! To this day, Linda remains one of my favorite people.

During those years I wrote and recorded a few songs at Linda's urging. None soared to the top, but I did collect a Gold Record for working with Don Henley on his big hit single *Dirty Laundry.* I also wound up with musician friends on the tennis court. John Thomas Griffith – lead guitarist and singer for the popular band Cowboy Mouth – and session player/bandleader Bob Goldstein joined our band of tennis players and we had great fun. Bob also wrote a great, albeit, satirical song titled "You Want Change You Got It" that targeted the 2016 presidential election with some sharply biting lyrics. I also produced a half hour television music special on PBS featuring our friends Stephanie Bettman and Luke Halpin. This amazingly gifted duo specializes in music that might best be described as Americana and they are great fun, as well.

Over the years, I also had become friends with Stephen Stills of the band Crosby, Stills & Nash. Stephen was a political junky and a fan of former President Jimmy Carter. At one point, I did a fun interview with Stephen for CNN to which I brought my favorite guitar – a 1955 Fender Telecaster signed to me by Leo Fender. I could almost see Stephen drooling. Another time, Stephen decided to host a fancy dinner with a very limited guest list that included two of my very different friends – singer/songwriter Delbert McClinton and Lee Atwater who happened to be the chairman of the Republican National Committee. Lee also was an outstanding guitar player. After dinner, Stephen suggested we adjourn to the "garage" where he kept his extensive guitar collection. The result was an ad hoc jam session during part of which Stephen played bottleneck guitar. Lee's two companions were a couple of GOP stiffs from Orange County in suits, button down shirts, ties and black shoes. But even they could not keep their toes from tapping as the jam session continued. Not long after, my daughter Courtney was born and Stephen became her godfather.

# CHAPTER 18

When I first moved to Los Angeles, a friend urged me to take up skiing. So, we went to Big Bear in the San Bernardino Mountains where I rode a lift for the first time and fell rather than skied my way down the hill. But I actually had a great time. I already was into camping and backpacking and the developing trend into cross country skiing caught my attention. First, however, the backpacking.

One of my earlier friends in Los Angeles was a doctor – Bob Rosenquist. We both lived in an apartment complex that was home to doctors who were completing their residencies at the USC-County Medical Center. The apartment complex had a swimming pool, sauna and tennis court and the tennis court had its own teaching pro. Bob and I and some others spent much of our time on that court. One of our closest friends was another tennis player – Rick Emerson who had been captain of the UCLA tennis team and spent some time on the pro tour. He had a 100 mph serve with a wooden racket! One day, I arranged a doubles match between Bob and Rick on one side and Joe Blatchford of Peace Corps and Wimbledon fame and I on the other side. Joe suggested that I should concentrate on defending the doubles alleys and he would take care of the rest. And did he ever! We swept the match. For Bob, Rick and I, it was a demonstration of what it is like to play in the big leagues – an arena well out of our reach.

Bob Rosenquist in the Eastern Sierra

Bob and I took so many backpacking trips together that they are a bit jumbled in my mind. I know we packed through much of the eastern Sierra, as well as Mineral King and Yosemite and Kings Canyon. We also did Lamoille Canyon in Nevada couple of times and chunks of Idaho including the Big Horn Crags, the Sawtooths, the White Clouds and other mountain locales. We packed into the Wind River Range in Wyoming and more. On our way into the White Clouds, we were confronted by an older woman waving a shotgun and telling us to move along because we were on her mining property. We picked up our pace and moved on. Shortly thereafter, we came upon the remains of an old airplane that clearly had crashed on the mountainside a long time ago. Fishing on that trip was amazing. We had trout for breakfast and dinner most days. A few years later, I repeated part of that trip as a multi-day solo backpack and got caught in a summer blizzard that forced me to hole up in my tent for a couple of days while dining on a can of sardines and crackers. On my way out, I stopped by a stream in which to soak my tired feet and suddenly a Clark's Nutcracker flew from a nearby branch and snatched up one of my socks. I was surprised this flying camp robber did not choke on the days old sock.

On our backpack into the Big Horn Crags, the fishing also was excellent and so was the scenery. But the highlight was on our way back home. The New York Times had listed the bowling alley in the small town of Challis as having the best onion rings in North America. This we had to check out. So, we pulled up to the bowling alley, walked in and asked for an order of onion rings. We put them in a bag, got back in the car and out on the highway. Then, we opened the big and each dug out an onion ring. We looked at each other and not a word was spoken as, by common consent, we hung a U-turn, headed back to the bowling alley and ordered a bunch more onion rings to sustain us on our drive back toward Nevada. Mmmmmm. Good!

Some years later, the Blackburn, Rosenquist and Emerson adults gathered for camping in the Sawtooths. As is always the case, the setting was awesome. My wife Gloria and I horsepacked into Alice Lake – one of the most beautiful backcountry lakes to be found anywhere. The trip had many highlights but, near the end, we were driving down a dirt road when suddenly – there on the road ahead – was a wolf. It was focused on a deer grazing nearby. It was my first sighting of a wolf in the wild.

Another time, we were on a backpack in the Ruby Mountains in Nevada. The Rubies look like someone cut a chunk out of the Sierra and dropped it into eastern Nevada. It is a pretty neat mountain range. We had planned for a multi-day pack. However, on the second day, it snowed. And snowed and snowed. Even the dog insisted on sleeping in the tent. Not a big deal, except the dog had a horrible attack of the farts. Had it not been snowing so hard, we might have moved out and left the tent to the dog.

However, in any season, the Sierra is home. Once, Bob and I climbed the steep trail out of Mineral King to get deep into the back country when a storm suddenly erupted. We ducked into a cave like depress in the side of the mountain and, not thinking, I stood straight up, hit my head on the ceiling and knocked myself out. The rest of the trip was pretty good, though. The Nine Lakes Basin is absolutely spectacular.

Somewhere in the Backcountry

I backpacked and skied over much of the Sierra, as well as part of the Canadian Rockies, Nevada, Utah and Idaho. I became very serious about cross country skiing and its cousin back country skiing and ski mountaineering. Indeed, I even went to Mountaineering School and earned the well-deserved green patch that remains sewed onto my favorite skiing jacket. In addition to improving skiing techniques, the school taught route finding, building igloos and snow caves and avoiding avalanches. The latter became a challenge. I joined a very small group of back country skiers who flew by helicopter into the Canadian Rockies and set up camp beneath towering summit of Mt. Assiniboine which soars more than 5000 feet above Lake Magog where we base camped. Mt. Assiniboine is known as the Matterhorn of Canada. We spent several days exploring the area and then began the trek down and across to the town of Banff. On the second day, we were carefully crossing an area prone to avalanches and I was bring up the rear when the slope let go. Fortunately, my training kicked in and I started using swimming motions in the snow to keep my head up and avoid being totally buried. When everything settled down, only my head was sticking out of the snow which had settled around me like cement. The other members of the group started digging and eventually they were able to free me from the frigid grip of the surrounding snow. The rest of the trip back to civilization was uneventful. But another avalanche lay in the future.

Back in the Eastern Sierra, Bob and I linked up with our good friend Marty Hornick for another adventure. Marty, who was a senior member of the U.S. Forest Service supervising the Inyo National Forest, is well known in mountaineering circles and a very strong and tough individual. He has held records in climbing Mt. Whitney as well as setting a wide range of ski touring and mountaineering achievements. He also boasted one of the best outdoor hot tubs in the Sierra. He is great pals with near legendary mountaineer Doug Robinson. There is no one I would want to be with more in the back country than those guys if things started to go wrong.

Marty Hornick Approaching University Peak Summit

One spring, Marty suggested that we climb University Peak –
a 13,600-foot summit in the Sierra. The idea was that we would
climb the peak so that we could ski down. As we paused to catch
our breath, an eagle circled overhead for a couple of turns and then
headed off toward Yosemite. We took that as a good sign and had a
delightful time skiing down to the base of the mountain.

Marty and Doug and I first met at Rock Creek Winter Lodge
in the Sierra wilderness area. To get there, you had to be able to ski in
and ski out. Over the course of several years, I spent a lot of time in
Rock Creek Canyon and loved every minute of it no matter what the
season. In addition to Marty and Doug, several other advanced ski-

ers and climbers also could be found at the lodge. One of them was international women's Olympic skier Sue Burak who taught a clinic in telemark turns – the somewhat difficult turn unique for the use of cross country skis going downhill. Under her guidance, it became my favorite turn.

Jumping a few years forward, one lovely early spring, Bob, Marty and I decided to attempt skiing from Rock Creek to the Mammoth Mountain ski area or, at the very least, to Convict Lake. Under the best of circumstances, this would be a somewhat dicey trip because it crossed some serious avalanche areas and required a bunch of ups and downs. Still, the weather seemed promising and we set off spending much of the first day climbing up to Half Moon Pass – a small pass that was aptly named and which would open up the route as we headed north. We crossed the pass – which gave us a great view of the route ahead – and dropped down into a somewhat sheltered area where we would spend the first night. As soon as our tents were set up, we headed up to survey the route ahead and Marty did some cornice jumping. A cornice might best be described as an outcropping of snow on the side of a mountain and some people – Marty among them – thought jumping off one would be fun. And, for him, it was. After that break in the action, we spent some more time scouting the route ahead and then headed back to camp for dinner before tucking ourselves into our sleeping bags. Sometime during the night, I heard noises and poked my head out of the tent. It was snowing and snowing hard. By morning, it was a blizzard. Visibility was limited and we were unable to go anywhere. In addition, the conditions were an invitation to avalanche country. We hunkered down for a day and, when the snow finally stopped, took a hard look at the conditions. None of the options were good. Going forward bordered on suicidal. Going back over Half Moon Pass was not very appealing either. However, we decided to wait until very early the next morning and retrace our steps back over the pass. The idea was to cross the pass before the sun warmed up the snow. So, very early the next morning we broke camp and slogged up and over the pass. Conditions were not very good on the pass. Marty suggested that we take off one after another and ski down to the tree line and get in among the trees. And that is what we did. Shortly thereafter, while we were still catching our breath, the slope broke loose, and an avalanche roared past us and down into Rock Creek Canyon. Had we not been protected by the trees, the situation might have been dire.

A few years earlier, I embarked on one of the Sierra ski trips of a lifetime. David Beck – a well-known and highly regarding skiing guide and mountaineer – wanted to lead a group of backcountry skiers on a test of a route that would be the highest possible guided crossing of the Sierra on skis. He had skied the route himself in 1975 and believed it would become the Sierra Haute Route similar but more dramatic than the European Haute Route. I had met David before a couple of times and expressed interest in joining the group. That was easier said than done. You had to pass a skiing test devised by David, as well as display general knowledge of backcountry travel. The ski test took up an entire morning on pretty good snow above Mammoth Lakes. The rest mostly was conversation.

A few days later, we gathered at the Symmes Creek trailhead to start the adventure and David limited everyone to 30 pounds in their packs, including food and other necessities. Then we started the slog up the 5000-foot climb to Anvil Camp. The sun hammered us every step of the way and it was good that Symmes Creek ran beside us on its way down to the Owens Valley. By the time we reached Anvil camp, most of us were teetering on the edge of exhaustion. Nonetheless, we pitched our tents and set up camp before collapsing next to a roaring fire. Later, sitting on the edge of the camp and look-ing out over the darkened land 5000 feet below, the small lights that flickered served as exclamation points marking the end of the day. Doug Robinson and Marty Hornick worked out an easier route that took a bit longer but also was less exhausting. They would start out of Onion Valley above the town of Independence and then ski north to Shepherd Pass. Made sense to me.

The next day, we headed toward Shepherd Pass, often consid-ered among the most dangerous of all the Sierra passes. As we were climbing up toward the pass, I lost an edge on my skis and started sliding toward a 100 foot drop off. Training again kicked in. I used my ski poles to self-arrest and came to a stop not far from a fatal plunge. David lowered a rope to me and I wrapped it around while he pulled me up. Then, we journeyed on up and over Milestone Pass slightly more than 13,000 feet high – the highest pass in the Sierra. Compared to Shepherd Pass, Milestone Pass was relatively easy. David's then-wife Susan insisted that she be allowed to guide and, despite deep reservations, she took over and promptly skied us into a dead-end canyon which forced us to climb back out in order to continue our journey. The views were spectacular. To the south loomed the summit of Mt. Whitney followed by a parade of peaks stretching up to us and beyond.

Skiing conditions were at their very best as we soared over the high Sierra and down to the Tablelands – a rolling series of slopes and bumps in Sequoia National Park. This is an awesome place to ski and I packed up into it a couple of other times in other years just to spend a couple of days playing in the varied terrain. Fun! Fun! Fun! On this first trip, though, we spent a night at the Pear Lake Hut in Sequoia and then headed on down a rather icy descent into the Wolverton Parking lot in the park, spending our last night actually in some park cabins taking showers and having dinner before returning to our homes.

Mammoth Mountain is the Eastern Sierra skiing destination. Founded by Dave McCoy in 1953, this ski area – along with its second ski location June Mountain—is a short day's drive from Los Angeles and very popular. My children Dylan and Courtney cut their skiing and snowboarding teeth on those slopes. At one point, Dave McCoy offered a few of us backcountry skiers free passes if we would ski Mammoth on our cross-country skis and make use of the traditional and graceful telemark turn used by backcountry skiers. Seemed like a great idea to me. This became part of the Mammoth skiing lessons program. One day, mountaineer Alan Bard – known as the Great Bardini, photographer Galen Rowell and I were skiing Mammoth when Galen made a turn and plunged face first into a snowbank. In typical Galen fashion, he leaped back up and declared, "That was fun. Let's do it again!"

I can't leave the subject of skiing without returning to Idaho. The state's chief guide was Joe Leonard – another man of near leg-endary feats. He and his wife Sheila lived in Stanley, Idaho, at the base of the Sawtooth Mountains – some of the most beautiful mountain country in the United States. In the mid-Seventies, Joe decided to start a hut to hut ski system in the Sawtooths. This meant hauling all sorts of material and equipment into the locations for three yurt-style canvas huts. That included cast iron stoves and one large horse trough that theoretically would become a wilderness hot tub. Joe, who I had gotten to know previously, asked me to join him in what would amount to an inaugural run of the hut system. Everything was pretty much in place and a couple of local skiers also joined us for the hut tour. Except for the weather, it was a good trip. We got hammered a couple of times by storms and one day three friends from Sun Valley skied in to join us and we put the wilderness hot tub into a test mode. Actually, it worked pretty well so long as someone kept stoking the wood fire underneath. The only challenge was getting back into the tent. Warm body. Cold air. Yiiiiks. Another time, Joe decided we should see some mountain lions which are plentiful in the Sawtooths. So, we skied out into the wilderness, set up camp and waited. Saw fresh cat tracks every morning but never saw a big cat.

**Joe Leonard Sawtooth Mountains Idaho**

Another year, Joe decided that a group of us should ski into the White Clouds and base camp at Castle Peak – the highest mountain in that range. Plans were made. Skis were prepped and, right on schedule, we headed into the mountains with the big peak in our line of sight. However, there was one small problem. The snow had turned into the winter equivalent of sawdust. Even on skis, we would sink down almost knee deep. For three ugly days, we struggled through that impossible snow and finally decided that our food would wear out before we got to Castle Peak. And we would wear out, too. But Joe had an idea. Singer/songwriter Carole King owned Robinson Bar Ranch somewhere not too far away. The sprawling ranch was spread over 128 acres with a log ranch house, cabins, a recording studio and two heated swimming pools. It was closed in winter, although a dirt road more or less was kept open for access from the highway. So, we struggled and straggled all the way to the ranch, took off our sweat stained clothes and plunged into the heated pool. Unknown to us, a new chef had arrived from France to cook at the ranch. He never had heard of anyone skiing in the back country, let alone seen anyone doing it. But, there we were, unshaven, sweaty, smelly and weird looking. Joe used a phone to call his wife and the wife of one of our colleagues – a bearded Alaskan named John – to come and collect us. Meanwhile, the chef kept pouring us French wine. Before too long, the two ladies joined us in the pool and more wine was poured. We were getting seriously blitzed. At one point, I put my arm around John's wife, looked her in the eye and declared to her "John you sure have a pretty cute wife". Everyone thought that was hysterical. But there would be more. The women decided we had to return to Stanley. So, we staggered out of the pool, got dressed and headed for the truck they had driven in. There was not a lot of room and, somehow, I wound up back in the bed of the truck with the dog. And Joe insisted on driving. Now the dirt road was narrow and the bridge over the Salmon River was equally narrow. "No worries," declared Joe as he stepped on the gas and drove directly into the barn where the hay was stored for the winter. Bales of hay flew everywhere as the dog and I kept ducking. Then, we popped out the other side of the barn and onto the dirt road. Somehow, we did not plunge into the river. Whichever gods protect fools in the mountains had their hands full that day. Eventually, we wound up back in Stanley and, to this day, I credit that as a minor (or major) miracle.

# CHAPTER 19

Safely back in California, my telephone rang in the summer of 1979 and the NBC bureau chief was on the line telling me to grab a bag and that a courier would pick me up and take me to LAX where I would catch a plane to Managua, Nicaragua. I was aware that a revolution was underway with the rebel Sandinistas seeking to overthrow the current dictator – Anastasio Somosa Debayle – whose family had ruled the Central American nation for 46 years. The courier arrived with a package of background material and a briefcase containing $10, 000 in cash that I was to deliver to the field producer in Managua – Don Critchfield – to cover the costs of bribes and paying various taxi drivers. Just a couple of weeks earlier, an ABC News correspondent had been shot and killed by government troops near the Managua city limits. That killing caused the U.S. government to withdraw its limited support for the Somosa regime. Critchfield met me at the airport and we were driven to what amounted to a press compound. Shortly thereafter, I was on a pay phone to the news desk in New York when a group of Sandinistas came around the corner waving their automatic weapons. I told the person on the phone in New York that if he heard a bunch of loud noises then I would be in deep trouble. Then, I started shouting "prensa!prensa" which is Spanish for "press". Apparently, that worked because the rebels turned away and shot up a nearby café – doing some damage but causing no harm to anyone. We were located not far from the presidential palace and clearly were in a war zone. Within a matter of days, Somosa called us all in to his bunker where he delivered a rambling speech, waved around what appeared to be a gold-plated revolver and then got on a waiting government airplane for his escape flight to Miami. Needless to say, most Nicaraguans were happy to see him go even though Cuba and the Soviet Union soon became supporters of the newly formed Sandinista government. That support came mostly by default. The new government in Manuaga had made it clear they were open to a relationship with the United States. But President Jimmy Carter unfortunately and unwisely would have none of it. Before long, I was back at the Managua airport to catch a flight home. The plane had made a stop earlier and, when I boarded, I noticed an empty seat next to a young woman who it turned out spoke some English. However, after we landed in Los Angeles, she asked if I would mind carrying her extra bag through customs as a favor. Strongly suspecting that she was carrying marijuana or some other illegal substance, I politely but firmly declined. I never saw her again.

On my return to Los Angeles, I was asked by a fellow member of our Friday Group folks if I would do her a favor. Without hesitating, I said "sure" and she said that she was writing a book – a biography—and that the subject of the book was staying at her apartment. So, would I check in on her? Of course I said, since she lived not too far from me. Then she said she needed to tell me that the subject of her book was Leslie Van Houten – a member of the Manson family who was out on parole while being in court. Since I had been off covering a presidential campaign, I actually knew very little about the Manson clan but now I was kind of stuck because I already had agreed to keep an eye on Leslie. So, we arranged for me to meet young Leslie and I was startled by her demure appearance and behavior. Leslie was nothing like what I had expected. She was very quiet but also clearly very intelligent. At the same time, I was not enthused about essentially babysitting a convicted killer. And I had no desire to spend several days cooped up in my friend's apartment. So, with the tentative approval of Leslie's attorney, I took the young woman on some tours of Los Angeles.

There was much she never had seen or experienced. We went to an outdoor birthday party in a lovely park. And we went roller skating in the Venice Beach area. It was there that we linked up with

Linda Ronstadt and Nicolette Larson and had an interesting chat until Leslie revealed who she was. As both women later said, Leslie was nothing like what they expected. Then, my book writing friend returned and took charge of Leslie. Some weeks later, I was summoned to testify at Leslie's court hearing which really had become something of a kangaroo court series of hearings. I responded to questions that my relatively brief time with Leslie had revealed no sign of the troubled young woman who had fallen prey to Charles Manson's evil influence. Clearly, prison had left its mark on Leslie but not all of that was negative and Leslie went on to become a highly respected leader among the women inmates, working with them to improve their lives and rejoin society in a constructive way. A growing group of people, including highly respected Associated Press crime reporter Linda Deutsch, has argued for some time that she should be paroled and the Parole Board has agreed but no governor, as of this writing, ever has signed off on the parole recommendation.

There were some moments at NBC that remain firmly in my memory. In those days, we had a wonderful program called NBC News Overnight hosted by Linda Ellerbee –one of those colleagues who you never forget. By its very nature, the show often featured interviews with musicians and others in the entertainment world. One day, singer Michael McDonald came to the studios to be interviewed. Now it happened that our production assistant at that time – an attractive young woman by the name of Kathy Riggins – had a huge crush on McDonald. However, she did not know that McDonald was in the building. After we finished the interview, I told him that Kathy was a huge fan and would he mind saying "hello" to her on the way out. "Sure", he said. So, we walked down the hall and I point Kathy out to him. McDonald walked up to her desk, said "Hello Kathy" and then leaned over and kissed her! Briefly, I thought we might need to call the EMTs but she did recover.

However, her story continues. NBC Nightly News sometimes had to be updated for the West Coast and a correspondent from time to time would be summoned to race in from home or where ever and cut into Tom Brokaw's show. On this occasion, I was the correspondent on tap. I received a phone call, grabbed a coat and tie and raced to the studios where were not far away. With my makeup on and the script on the teleprompter, I was ready to go when Kathy, who was working as the floor producer, walked up to me and planted a big kiss on my lips! In my ear, I could hear the director counting down – 10, 9, 8 .7, 6, 5, 4—and, at the 3 second mark, Kathy stepped out of the camera shot and I delivered the update live without missing a beat. And it still remains one of my favorite updates.

Then, there was the very famous Jack Perkins story. Jack was an NBC Correspondent based in Tokyo. Eventually, the day came when Jack was asked to return home which was on the West Coast. Jack said "fine" and sent a telegram back which approximately said, in part, "Assume you will pay to have me and my junk returned back to the states." And the folks in New York said that would be fine. But Jack meant his words literally and NBC wound up paying to have Jack's Japanese junk (a small boat) shipped back to the United States.

# CHAPTER 20

As promised, here is the return to politics. In 1976, Ronald Reagan – then governor of California – had challenged incumbent President Gerald Ford for the Republican presidential nomination. As Richard Nixon's Vice President, Ford had succeeded Nixon when the then-President was forced to resign over the Watergate scandal. However, Ford – an eminently likeable man – was now the president and Republican voters were not really unhappy with him. Also, Reagan – although governor of California – was looked upon with some suspicion because he had been a Hollywood actor and a former Democrat as well as a union leader. Ford – a pipe smoking Midwesterner – tended to miss-speak which sometimes made him look foolish. I remember sitting with a small group of reporters interviewing Ford some years earlier when he famously declared, "If Abraham Lincoln were alive today, he would turn over in his grave." Our giggles were barely suppressed.

Ford had been an outstanding college football player at the University of Michigan, but critics often said that he had failed to wear a helmet when playing the game – falsely implying that Ford was none too bright. Truthfully, Gerry Ford and his wife Betty were genuinely decent people and well liked in Washington. Nonetheless, Reagan took a run at the nomination and one of his then-aides – Dana Rohrbacher – later went on to become a member of Congress. Success in 76 was not in the cards for the governor of California. But the stage clearly was set for a retry in 1980. Also in the wings on the Democratic side was Ted Kennedy.

It was no secret that Kennedy and President Jimmy Carter did not hold each other in very high regard. It would have been hard to find such very different personalities. Kennedy – an outspoken liberal and a fiery speaker – was often hail fellow, well met. He and I had become friends in the late Sixties and the Seventies. As previously noted, he had given his blessing to the Robert F. Kennedy Journalism Awards program and we spoke from time to time on the telephone. In late 1979, Kennedy sat down for what became a cringe worthy interview with Roger Mudd on CBS. Because the Kennedy family considered Mudd to be a friendly reporter, they mistakenly thought he would go easy on the soon to be candidate. But that was not Roger's style. The questions were tough and, when he asked EMK to deliver an explanation of why he should be president, Kennedy's rambling and unfocused answer was a disaster. As the campaign got into full swing in early 1980, Kennedy continued to struggle. In Iowa – site of the first political caucuses every four years –Kennedy struggled to find his footing. At one point, he referred to the working farmers as "fam farmilies" instead of farm families. President Jimmy Carter's popularity was at a low ebb for a variety of reasons, including his handling of the Iran hostage crisis involving American hostages. But he managed to win several primaries while Kennedy suffered from the Chappaquiddick accident that took the life of Mary Jo Koepechne.

President Jimmy Carter Shakes Kennedy's
Hand at Democratic Convention

While campaigning in Chicago, he had to wear a bulletproof vest because of a series of assassination threats. I liked none of what I saw on this Kennedy campaign and, when we stopped for a couple of nights in Los Angeles, I asked Ted's press secretary Dick Drayne for some private personal minutes with his boss. My request was granted and I sat down looked Ted in the eye and told him the campaign was not working out and he was not looking good and should pull the plug. He thanked me for my input and, in a great display of how much influence I really had, he continued on campaigning all the way to the Democratic National Convention where he finally conceded defeat but refused to raise Jimmy Carter's hand in the traditional show of convention support. It was at that convention that Kennedy delivered what many believe to have been his greatest speech ever. He summed it up by declaring, "*For me, a few hours ago, this campaign came to an end. For all those whose cares have been our concern, the work goes on, the cause endures, the hope still lives, and the dream shall never die.*"After that, Kennedy became a giant in the U.S. Senate and one of its most respected leaders. He accurately was described as the "Lion of the Senate" In 2008, Kennedy endorsed Barack Obama and said it was "time again for a new generation of leadership." Later that year, following a pair of strokes, he was diagnosed with a malignant brain tumor. Nonetheless, Kennedy insisted on appearing during the first night of the 2008 Democratic National Convention on August 25, 2008, where a video tribute to him was played. Introduced by his niece, Caroline Kennedy, the senator said, "It is so wonderful to be here. Nothing – nothing – is going to keep me away from this special gathering tonight."[1] He then delivered a speech to the delegates (which he had to memorize, as his impaired vision left him unable to read a teleprompter) in which, reminiscent of his speech at the 1980 Democratic National Convention, he said, "*this November, the torch will be passed again to a new generation of Americans. So, with Barack Obama and for you and for me, our country will be committed to his cause. The work begins anew. The hope rises again. And the dream lives on.*" The dramatic appearance and speech electrified the convention audience, as Kennedy vowed that he would be present to see Obama inaugurated. Ted and I stayed in touch by phone and brief notes up to when he became too weak to carry on such exchanges. He died at his home in Hyannis Port, Massachusetts, at the age of 77. And I miss him to this day.

# CHAPTER 21

Meanwhile, other Democrats were busy seeking the White House in the Eighties. Although several Democrats sought the 1984 nomination, the contest came down to a close fight between Walter Mondale, who had been Jimmy Carter's vice president, and Colorado Senator Gary Hart. But, before going there, this is a good place to time travel back to 1980 and Ronald Reagan's successful run for the White House.

After losing to Ford in 1976, Reagan was the odds on favorite to win the GOP nomination in 1980. He had a lot going for him as a movie star, governor and campaign experience. He also had a very good team lead by veteran Republican political strategist Stu Spencer – one of the truly decent men in professional politics. Longtime Reagan aide Mike Deaver became the man always at Reagan's side. Lyn Nofziger – the very savvy press secretary – was there every day and most nights. Lyn often came up with repeatable quotes. Among the favorites was, "The executive branch has grown too strong. The judicial branch too arrogant and the legislative branch too stupid." Lyn's first name was Franklyn but all who really knew him always called him Lyn. And, equally important, Reagan had a dedicated partner in his wife Nancy whose influence often was under-rated. I had gotten to know the Reagans and their staff in the early Seventies and, on a personal level, genuinely liked them.

So, it is 1980 and Reagan is in the race. For some of us – including such camera crew stalwarts as Jim White – arguably the best network cameraman at the time – and Bob DeServi from the Chicago bureau – it was on the road again. From time to time, we were joined by the wonderful Linda Ellerbee out of New York. My NBC colleague Chris Wallace – now working at Fox News – from Washington, D.C., was on board. And highly respected senior producer Ray Cullin – known as the Silver Fox by his colleagues – from our Burbank Bureau was there every day. Reagan was opposed by George H.W. Bush – the scion of the Bush family. Bush was a member of internationalist organizations – such as the Trilateral Commission – that often drew criticism from conservatives. One of the hysterically funny moments of the Reagan campaign occurred around that issue.

We had made a stop in Texas – I think it was Houston – and Reagan had agreed to appear live on a local news program that evening. The traveling crew would watch from a pre-arranged hanger location with a video feed. As Reagan came down the steps from the campaign plane, the local reporter rush up to him and demanded, "Governor, why are you a member of the Trilateral Commission? Reagan, a bit taken aback, replied, "Well, actually, I am not a member of the Trilateral Commission. George Bush is a member of the Trilateral Commission." The reporter paused a moment and then asked, "Governor Reagan why aren't you a member of the Trilateral Commission?" Reagan's answer was lost amid the howls of laughter and derision directed at that poor, unprepared reporter.

For the most part, Ronald Reagan was a decent, open man who genuinely liked people and sometimes even liked reporters. He also had a very good sense of humor. Usually, when the campaign plane landed at a designated stop, there would be a line of local officials to greet and welcome the candidate. Sometimes, there were bands, too. From time to time, I would rush off the plane very quickly – assuming there were no expected news events – and work my way into the line of greeters. I would don a sport coat or something that looked reasonable appropriate and, when Reagan reached my place in line, I would – with a very straight face – welcome him to Bimidji or Little Rock or where ever we happened to be. He seemed to get a kick out of these small pranks. Initially, Nancy Reagan was less amused but began smiling as the campaign wore on. Once, I borrowed a hat from a member of a Mariachi band in Arizona and popped up in front to greet Reagan on behalf of the band. He actually broke out laughing. One of the better moments took place on a commercial flight from Boston to Los Angeles. I no longer recall why we were flying commercial that day. However, I noticed that a doctor friend of mine from Los Angeles – Bob Swinney – was also getting on the plane with a large box of live lobsters under his arm. I kept an eye on him and when he got up to go to the restroom, I stole the box of lobsters and hid it under Lyn Nofsiger's seat. When Bob returned to his seat, he noticed that the lobsters had gone missing and began a frantic search of the overhead bins. No luck. After he settled back in his seat, a flight attendant delivered a note to Bob saying that the lobsters were being held for ransom by the Lobster Liberation Army. By now Bob was totally baffled. An hour or so, probably longer, into the flight, a

Secret Service agent got on the speakers and said that he understood some very valuable items had gone missing. He added, "I want to assure everyone on board this plane that no one has gotten either on or off the aircraft since we took off from Boston." Many people visited Bob to display mock sympathy. Then, as we started to approach Los Angeles, Reagan rose from his seat and walked down the aisle with the box of lobsters under his arm. He stopped by Bob's seat and said, "Someone seems to have left a valuable campaign contribution to me in this box. However, it is illegal for me to accept anonymous campaign contributions. I understand you have suffered a serious personal loss. So, I am passing this contribution on to you." Then, he gave Bob the classic Reagan grin and turned about and walked back to his seat in the front cabin.

During our chartered campaign flights, Nancy Reagan would stand up as the plane took off and she would attempt to roll an orange down the aisle. The goal was for the orange to make it all the way to the back of the plane. That proved quite challenging, but she did it often with a smile on her face. All of us knew that she was trying to soften her image with us and that may have been even more challenging. At one point, she referred to reporters as "vampires" and the next day I hung a black rubber bat over my seat and attached a button that read "Working Newsman."

Nearly all of our chartered flights were on United Airlines and before long the flight crew – all young women – had been adopted as friends of the campaign team. That did not in any way suggest or imply that their behavior broke the bounds of professionalism. They worked hard and all of us – press as well as staff – really liked them. Then, one day, a temporary wire service reporter who was on board because the regular Associated Press guy was taking a couple of days off wrote an outrageous story implying that the flight crew was engaging in sex and other activities with the campaign staff and press. The reporter was immediately ostracized by all of us but, when the plane landed at our next stop, the entire crew abruptly was replaced with an all-male team. Everyone on board was furious. I was sitting near the front at that time and could hear Mike Deaver on the phone demanding to speak with the president of United Airlines.

When that official got on the phone, Mike verbally assaulted him in quite colorful language and demanded that our old flight crew be reinstated at our next stop. He concluded by telling the United Airlines president that, if our regular crew was not back then, United would be barred from ever flying government charters for as long as the Reagan Administration was in charge at the White House. Sure enough. The next morning our old crew was back and everyone was smiling.

It was more than a little evident that some members of the Reagan campaign staff and a few of the members of the travelling press were dabbling from time to time in marijuana smoking. I think almost everyone on the plane, including the Secret Service team, was aware of this somewhat suspect activity. After all, we're talking 1980. The only exceptions probably were the Reagans and maybe political strategist Stu Spencer. One evening, after a long campaign day, the distinct odor of pot began to swirl in the back of the plane. There was a Secret Service agent whom we all liked and referred to jokingly as Agent Orange. Well over six feet tall and one of three brothers all working in law enforcement, Agent Orange walked back to the rear of the aircraft and then turned and started to walk back toward the front. Then, speaking in a perfect accent of Sgt. Schultz from the cast of the popular TV series *Hogan's Heroes*, Agent Orange announced, "I hear nozzing. I see nozzing. I smell nozzing." The cabin erupted in an outburst of laughter.

I can't leave the Reagan campaign without telling about this impromptu caper. Linda Ellerbee, Ray Cullin and the rest of us were staying at the Guest Quarters on Pennsylvania Avenue in DC when we got word that our campaign charter would be preparing soon for a flight to somewhere. So, Linda and Ray thought it would be a great idea to create our own motorcade without the Secret Service or other police. So, some flashing lights were put on the lead car and we all got in line and barreled onto the freeway leading to Dulles International Airport. Things were going well and we all were having a great time when a Virginia Highway Patrol unit passed us going in the other direction on the other side of the divided highway. We could see the driver's expression which clearly said "Motorcade? What motorcade?" We stepped on the gas and raced into the restricted area of the airport where a Secret Service agent opened the gates to let us through to the campaign plane. Minutes later the Highway Patrol officer arrived at the gate but the federal agents would not let him pass. And we all had a good story to tell.

# CHAPTER 22

Reagan rather easily won the GOP nomination and then chose his defeated opponent – George H.W. Bush – as his Vice President. They made a bit of an odd couple. Bush was a classic example of New England upper class despite having represented Texas in Congress and Reagan was a classic example of more laid-back California. But both were tough politicians. Jimmy Carter was running for re-election as president and the race shaped up as fairly even. The two men met for only one debate and that was held in Cleveland. Reagan had criticized Carter for misrepresenting his record and, when Carter then accused Reagan of opposing Medicare, the Californian turned toward him and said, "There you go again." Those words became something of a political catch phrase. But there was more. During the debate, the issue of nuclear weapons came up and Carter said, "I had a discussion with my daughter, Amy, the other day, before I came here, to ask her what the most important issue was." The problem was that Amy was only 13 years old at the time. I instinctively felt that his comment was a political disaster and said so to some of the other reporters. Turned out that I was right and Reagan went on to win the election.

During the next eight years, I saw a lot of Reagan and his team as they often vacationed in California, frequently staying in Santa Barbara no far from Reagan's Rancho del Cielo mountain retreat. From time to time, I also was in Washington covering the Reagan White House. The California ties continued to play a role and I managed some scoops. In those days, access to the staff offices in the White House was fairly relaxed. Early one evening, as I was preparing to leave for the day, I decided to poke my head into the office of White House Counsellor Edwin Meese – a San Diego attorney and longtime Reagan supporter. Meese – a genial man – waved me on in to his office and poured both of us a drink from a bottle he had stashed in a desk drawer. We chatted briefly and suddenly the phone on Meese's desk rang. He told me it was the Secretary of Defense and they talked for several minutes. Meese than hung up the phone and told me that U.S. troops were arriving on the island of Granada to rescue a bunch of Americans who were studying at the medical school there and to take other actions. We agreed that I would sit on the story until he gave me a heads up that the situation was under control. He did so a couple of hours later and I broke the story that the United States had invaded Grenada.

Earlier, President Reagan had begun issuing warnings about the threat posed to the United States and the Caribbean by the "Soviet-Cuban militarization" of the Caribbean. He cited as evidence the excessively long airplane runway being built, as well as intelligence sources indicating increased Soviet interest in the island. Reagan said that the 9,000-foot (2,700 m) runway and the numerous fuel storage tanks were unnecessary for commercial flights, and that evidence pointed that the airport was to become a Cuban-Soviet forward military airbase.[20]

On May 29th, the Point Salines International Airport was officially renamed the Maurice Bishop International Airport, in honor of the slain pre-coup leader Maurice Bishop by the Government of Grenada. The main objectives on the first day of the invasion were the capture of the Point Salines Airport, to permit the 82nd Airborne Division land reinforcements on the island; and release of the American students who were under house arrest. Although heavily criticized by the international community and some members of Congress, the American people seemed mostly to support the action.

At another point, Dick Allen – the National Security Advisor – came up to me on the White House lawn as I was preparing for a live shot and said, "The NSC (National Security Council) meeting just ended and we have solved the Middle East problem." I replied, "Really. How are you doing that?" And he said, "We are going to nuke the entire area and then have Haliburton pave it over." Some months later, over the Reagan's annual Christmas/New Year party in Palm Springs, I received a call from a top Californian in the White House about Dick Allen, who had come under severe criticism for accepting some gifts. I was told reliably that Allen would be resigning the next day. We went live from Palm Springs and beat everyone with the story.

No mention of the Reagan campaign and presidency is complete without a word or two about his chief political strategist – Stu Spencer. Without hesitation, I cite Stu as one of the most thoroughly decent and straight forward men I ever have had the privilege to know in the warped world of politics. His word always was good and his sense of humor seldom failed him. We need more like him on both sides of the aisle.

And that brings me back to the Reagan vacations in Santa Barbara. The Reagans owned a hilltop ranch above Santa Barbara – Rancho del Cielo, Ranch in the Sky. It was there that the Reagans would go when they were on a retreat or vacation and ride their horses. They genuinely loved the place. Senior White House staff members stayed at an upscale hotel on the beach while the press corps stayed in a nearby hotel in Santa Barbara and almost everything was low key. On most days, I would get up early enough to go for a three-mile run along the beach and still get back to the hotel in time for a bite of breakfast and the morning briefing which usually was conducted by White House Press Secretary Larry Speaks. While outside developments could interrupt the relative tranquility of the annual Reagan summer vacation, the basic plan was the president and his aides would try not to commit any newsworthy event. In fact, we usually would see the Reagans only a couple of times during the vacation – one of those being the annual press party hosted by the Reagans.

The annual party followed the same pattern every year. Reporters could invite one guest – family member, good friend, etc. The Reagans would walk through a line-up of staff and reporters and stop to shake hands and share a few words with each person – all of it off the record. Mostly, it was just a lot of informal fun with good food and drinks. The Reagan team always hired a good local rock band to provide music and, during one of the parties, I wound up on stage playing bass with the band on a couple of songs including Jackson Browne's *Stay*.

One year, however, I caused a small stir. I had invited my friend Nicolette Larson – the popular female rock star and pal of my friend Linda Ronstadt – as my guest. Nic was on tour but thought she would be close enough to Santa Barbara to make it to the party. At the last minute, however, plans fell apart and I was bemoaning my bad luck during a phone call with another longtime friend – actress June Lockhart. As it turned out, June was planning to drive up to Santa Barbara anyway and she volunteered to be my date. So, there we were, standing in the receiving line as Ronald and Nancy Reagan approached. When Reagan saw June his face lit up as though someone had just thrown a happy switch. Then, I noticed that Nancy Reagan was looking at me with undisguised anger. However, she managed a smile when it came time to shake hands. I had no idea what the issue was with her until later when June explained that she and Reagan used to do the USO tours to entertain the troops together. My basic reaction was "Ah Ha".

Nancy Reagan, Ronald Reagan, June Lockhart
and Me at Reagan Summer Party

Fortunately, Nancy Reagan decided to forgive me and that was important because a rather unusual situation had developed in which she had decided that there were only three reporters whom she could trust and I was one of them. This resulted in her sitting down with us for some off the record discussions that over time proved quite helpful in understanding some of the relationships both inside and outside the White House.

During one of the Santa Barbara vacations, I convinced NBC that it might be fun to record an interview in Santa Barbara with a pair of well-known musicians – my friend T Bone Burnett and his pal Elvis Costello.

**The Coward Brothers in Santa Barbara**

The two of them appearing as The Coward Brothers had recorded a song called *The Peoples Limousine* which poked fun at the rulers of Italy and elsewhere who claimed to love the proletariat but who also rode around in their own private limousine.

But the two of them started talking about how their music always was "stolen" by other musicians and that, as a result, they never got credit for their work. This was all done very tongue in cheek and they spoofed the Everly Brothers who they called the "Ever Brotherlies" and the Beach Boys and Elvis Presley and every sentence became more and more funny. Finally, I started to giggle and then the cameraman did and the sound person and soon we all were laughing helplessly. The folks at NBC loved it.

There were other interesting moments. At one point, a friendly Secret Service agent who was assigned to the security detail at the Reagan ranch told me how he had dozed off while sitting at his perimeter location. Then, he heard a sound and jerked awake only to find himself pretty much eye to eye with a mountain lion. He said the big cat spun around and took off but it took a while for him to get his heart beat back to normal.

One of the strangest moments came on March 30, 1981. My pal Bob Rosenquist and I had set off to ski across the upper part of Yosemite National Park by crossing Tuolumne Meadows on our cross-country skis. We had successfully reached the visitors Center which was firmly closed and banked with snow, when I noticed an old pay phone not far from the center's main building. Just for the heck of it, I skied over to the booth, kicked off my skis and wriggled my way inside. Much to my surprise, the phone had a dial tone and I decided to call the news desk in Washington to tell them where I was and that I was having a grand old time. The very first question before I hardly had chance to speak was to ask where I was. I answered and added "what's up?" The stunning answer—"Reagan's been shot." Also shot and very seriously wounded was Reagan's highly popular and much respected press secretary Jim Brady who eventually died as the result of his wounds. The most immediate question was how fast could I get back to Los Angeles and on to a plane to Washington? Flying in a helicopter to pick me up was not an option. So, Bob and I turned around and within a day managed to ski all the way out to where we had abandoned our car. Several hours later, I was back in the NBC Bureau in Burbank but by then plans had changed and I stayed in California doing reaction stories. Reagan, of course, survived and served out two full terms as president.

# CHAPTER 23

1984 was the year of a closely fought battle between former Vice President Walter Mondale and Senator Gary Hart of Colorado. Added to the mix was the Rev. Jesse Jackson – the second African American to seek the presidency. Cong. Shirley Chisholm was the first. Because of my previous experience, NBC decided I would rotate between all three campaigns. I often think of this as the year of near misses. I was on Walter Mondale's plane when it was hit by a service truck while on the runway. I was on Jesse Jackson's plane when it lost an engine in flight and on Gary Hart's plane when the right engine caught on fire on takeoff from Philadelphia. That was easily the scariest of the three as a 20-foot-long flame erupted from the engine and shot back to where it was totally visible from inside the plane. A number of people panicked and started ducking under seats, etc. My camera crew lead by Bob DeServi remained calm and cool and stood up and remained standing with their camera focused on Hart and his wife Lee until we landed safely back in Philadelphia. Equally impressive was the coolness shown by the Harts. They remained in their seats, holding hands while many about them were seriously losing their cool.

Gary Hart was an interesting candidate. He was an intellectual who gained much of his experience by helping manage George McGovern's successful run for the Democratic nomination in 1972. McGovern lost the general election in a landslide. But Hart learned a lot and put it to use in his own race for the White House. Of course, Fritz Mondale was no slouch either and their battle was interesting to watch. Rev. Jackson was the wild card.

Let's start with Jackson – known to his traveling press corps as "the Rev". Jackson was highly articulate and very charismatic. Most of his campaign events were aimed at the African American community. During at least part of the campaign NBC rented a limousine for the camera crew, producers and correspondents. I never quite understood why. Much to my delight, the lead producer on the NBC crew was the amazing Don Critchfield – last seen in Nicaragua. Critchfield – informally known as "Critch" – was the TV news producer personified. I recall a long and cold day in (I think) Iowa when Don disappeared for a while only to return with filet mignon steaks for everyone along with a fresh linen tablecloth and silverware and drinks. He never said where he got the goodies but no one complained. The second producer was A'lelia Bundles – a hardworking, smart and dedicated black woman from Washington and a graduate of Radcliff College. As for the limousine, sometimes "the Rev" rode in it, too.

Jackson had an on again, off again relationship with this accompanying press corps. He called us "alligators" which he defined as people who make up allegations. So, one day in Los Angeles, Critch bought a fluffy stuffed alligator and put it in the middle of the walkway that Jackson would have to use as he left the hotel. Jackson saw it. Laughed. And then kicked the stuffed alligator right over his waiting car.

The Jackson campaign stopped frequently at churches where the candidate would mix a campaign speech and a sermon into one package. He was especially popular with the church ladies who would cook up huge amounts of fried chicken, biscuits or potatoes and gravy in case the candidate might be hungry. Invariably, he and we were. Also, invariably, Jackson drew good crowds. In some respects, he was the Bernie Sanders of his day with a message that hammered the elite and spoke passionately about the problems of the disadvantaged. He said his goal was to create a Rainbow Coalition of people of all colors who had been left out of the life of mainstream America. Unfortunately, his campaign often was disorganized and usually short of funding. However, it never was boring. And he managed to win 21% of the popular vote in the Democratic primaries and caucuses.

In many ways, Gary Hart was the most exciting and interesting candidate in the presidential race in 1984. He was politically savvy, articulate, witty, good looking and, at 47, relatively young. An experienced member of the U.S. Senate, Hart already had a political record and some questions about his private life. On the campaign plane, his wife Lee often joined reporters in their ongoing card game – usually Gin Rummy – and she was well liked by the traveling press corps, many of whom were genuinely fond of her. But rumors circulated that Hart had been involved with other women, especially during their two marital separations. More fuel was added to those rumors when actor Warren Beatty – who had a well- known reputation for womanizing – joined the campaign plane on a semi-regular basis.

NBC News Correspondent Mary Nissenson—out of the Chicago Bureau – had been added to our campaign coverage team. However, Mary often seemed to think we should be covering her rather than Hart. Her prima donna attitude seriously offended the camera crew working with her. At one point, the crew put down their equipment on an airport tarmac and declared that if she got back on the plane then they would not get on. She also left little doubt that she would try to seduce Hart. Heaven knows, she tried – at one point standing on the arm of his plane seat and pretending to reach in an overhead bin while not wearing any underwear. But there is no reason to think that she was successful. She did better with Warren Beatty. In fact, she secretly flew to Paris with the campaigning actor for a long weekend. However, word leaked out as to where she was after news executives in New York started asking questions. I had a long conversation with the then Executive Vice President of the news division – former correspondent and longtime friend Tom Pettit – who asked whether the stories he was hearing about Mary were true. I replied that they were. He asked me to tell her to call him when I next saw her. A day or two later, she returned to the campaign and I passed along Tom's request. He asked her to fly back to New York which she did and that was the last we saw of her.

Hart made an effort to get along with most reporters, especially when he was walking along the California coast with his family or doing something else that tended to make for good video. Once, when he took them whitewater rafting, he called out over his shoulder, "I love danger." It would be four years later before we learned how much he loved risky business. Maybe I got a hint of it mid-way through his 1984 presidential campaign. He invited me to attend a private, off-the-record party in his hotel suite and I accepted the chance to see the Hart friends and family in an informal setting. What I saw was deeply dismaying. Hart clearly was drinking too much and I had the very distinct impression that drugs were circulating. Certainly, I picked up the odor of marijuana and felt that some harder drugs also may have been present. Also present were Hart's two children. The situation made me uncomfortable because I felt I would have to write about it if I stayed. So, I left. But the next day I confronted Hart's highly respected press secretary – Kathy Bushkin – and told her that if I ever witnessed such behavior in any circumstances I would immediately report it. Relations with Hart cooled off rather noticeably after that.

The Hart campaign also saw the birth of the Video Police. Bob DeServi decided that the press corps should have its own police. Badges were made and hats were designed. And Hart became the first honorary member.

If the Hart and Jackson campaigns were the spice of that election year, then Walter Mondale was the meatloaf. "Fritz" Mondale, as he was known, was the guy plugging along in the middle with your classic Democrat campaign. Mondale served as Vice President under Jimmy Carter and later would serve as U.S. Ambassador to Japan. Previously, he had represented the state of Minnesota in the U.S. Senate. There is no question that Mondale was smart, funny and very likeable. At one point during the primary campaign, I was invited to join longtime Kennedy political adviser Larry O'Brien and Mondale in Mondale's hotel suite. We chatted for a while and Mondale asked me for my views on the campaign. I replied that every time he put on a suit coat he always looked as though he had left the coat hanger in it and I suggested he loosen up and let the real person show through. O'Brien agreed but Fritz never quite managed to show up for the public events.

Meanwhile, Gary Hart had the political flash of a relative newcomer and appeared headed for an upset win. Then came their debate and Mondale very successfully borrowed a line from a Wendy's fast food commercial when he turned to Hart and asked, "Where's the beef?" which implied that Hart's campaign lacked substance. Mondale went on to win the nomination and surprised most observers when he picked New York Congresswoman Geraldine Ferraro to be his running mate. It was the first time that a woman would be on the national ticket. Selecting Ferraro gave the campaign some early momentum against Ronald Reagan who was bidding for a second term as president. However, the Democrats were unable to dent what critics often referred to as Reagan's Teflon coating that caused criticisms to bounce off him.

Early on, it appeared that Reagan might be vulnerable. His handling of the campaign's first debate was less than stellar and he appeared tired and somewhat disjointed. Some thought that Reagan's age – 73 – might work against him. However, Mondale handed Republicans a major campaign issue by promising that he would raise taxes to help balance the budget. Then came the second debate with Reagan. The president chose to address the age issue directly by saying, "*I want you to know that also I will not make age an issue of this campaign. I am not going to exploit for political purposes my opponent's youth and inexperience.*"

The audience laughed and so did Mondale. Reagan went on to win the election in a landslide.

As previously noted, I had and continue to have a high regard for the men and women of the Secret Service who work hard protecting the president, vice president and presidential candidates. And I enjoyed spending time with them. While traveling with Mondale, two incidents occurred. At one point, we needed to get to a telephone while the speech was underway. The agents led me to an office to which they were supposed to have access. However, the door was locked. I raised a series of eyebrows when I pulled out my American Express card and used it to pop open the door lock. The second occurrence somewhat raised my eyebrows. I was invited to join the agents for a party in the hotel after they went off duty. Right on schedule I showed up at the suite of rooms where the agents were staying only to be almost swept away by the strong fumes of marijuana that permeated the indoor atmosphere. I thought this could raise some issues down the road and that it would be better for all of us if I skipped the party. So, I left.

# CHAPTER 24

So, time for another break from politics and a return to music. During my years in Washington, I had become friends with some great musicians including the wonderful Lurlean Hunter, Ella Fitzgerald and Keter Betts. Keter was a brilliant bass player – contributing in a major way to introducing bossa nova jazz to the United States and elsewhere. But I first met him as the bassist in the band that backed the stunningly beautiful and talented singer Lurlean Hunter. Lurlean was an occasional guest at our house when she played Washington and we often hung out after her shows, usually with Keter Betts who introduced me to Ella Fitzgerald. When a new club opened in the District, Lurlean was the opening act for the place. I decided to host a table for the opening that included California Governor Pat Brown, Ethel Kennedy, Time Magazine's Hays Gorey and Kennedy advisor Frederick Dutton. During a break, Lurlean joined us at the table – much to the delight of my friends. She told us she was planning to open her own club on Chicago's south side. When I next spoke to her, she told me that the mob bosses in Chicago wanted to control her club and that she had refused to work with them. A short time later she disappeared and it was widely believed that she had been killed for her lack of cooperation with the mobsters. However, there also were reports that she suddenly had retired and was raising her family in Michigan.

Meanwhile, Ella Fitzgerald and I stayed in touch, including after I had moved to Los Angeles. One day she called me up to ask if I knew a song the title of which had escaped her. So, she sang the song to me over the phone. I do not remember the song, but

I do remember the singing. Later, a musical was developed around the songs featured by the Duke Ellington Band. The show – called Sophisticated Ladies – was to open in Century City and I had a ticket down near the front. There was an empty seat next to me. Shortly before the curtain was to go up, there was a rustling in my aisle and a voice said "Hey, Dan". It was Ella. She sat next to me through the entire show and quietly sang along with many of the Ellington tunes. I was absolutely in Heaven.

But there is more. A friend of mine – NBC News Producer Wendy Goldstein – had a crush on singer, songwriter and harmonica player Delbert McClinton. Delbert is a good guy and once coached John Lennon on how to play the harmonica. He also introduced me to singer and awesome guitarist Bonnie Raitt on whom I have had a crush for many years. Bonnie and I hung out in the green room during a couple of Delbert's shows and bumped into each other from time to time. So, Wendy asked me what I thought of Delbert and I told her that I liked him personally and also was a real fan of his music. A while later, Wendy informed me that she had met Delbert and magic happened and she would be marrying him. That may have been the best thing that ever happened to Delbert. Wendy untangled the various threads of his career and then they launched the concept of doing musical tours on an ocean liner. Those tours have been widely copied and wildly successful.

Meanwhile, NBC was bought by General Electric and it was not long before it became apparent that there was a new sheriff in the corporate world. Soon, the more senior correspondents in the Burbank bureau were pushed into early retirement and it was clear that more cuts were coming. As the ax continued to fall, it was not long that my head was on the block despite the best efforts of bureau chief Bob Eaton to save it. Fortunately, CNN rode to my rescue and opened a new chapter in my journalistic life. They also approved my continuing to write for various print outlets. It was at CNN that my interest in photography blossomed.

# CHAPTER 25

Initially, CNN gave me some room to explore subjects they might otherwise have ignored. For example – polar bears. I pitched them on the idea of a story about polar bears and the people who spend time and money to photograph them. I had noticed that famed photographer George Lepp was going to provide his expertise for a group of amateur photographers based out of Churchill, Manitoba, up near the Canadian arctic. So, we arranged to follow them around while doing some video shooting on our own. It also became the start of a long-lasting friendship between myself and George Lepp. His advice over the years contributed substantially to my own photography skills.

Shortly after arriving, I arranged to meet with the Canadian wildlife experts to get their comments and put together some interviews and updates involving their experts. When I asked for their initial advice, it was bluntly told, "Never forget that the polar bear not you is at the top of the food chain here." Needless to say, I took that advice to heart. We were equipped with a pair of former military landing vehicles for most of our transportation. These vehicles were large, sturdy and heavy. Really heavy. My team split into two groups – myself and a cameraman in the front vehicle and our producer and second cameraman in the second vehicle. One day, when we were doing some random searching for and shooting the bears, our big LVT suddenly lurched ahead by several feet. The producer in the second vehicle asked if we had felt that lurch and I replied "yes". I was told to look behind us. There stood a large male polar bear giving us his equivalent of the evil eye. I was told that he had walked up and slapped our vehicle with one of his front paws. Absolutely! They are top of the food chain!

**Polar Bear Mom & Cub**

The photo tourism people usually ride in what are called Tundra Buggies which sit up several feet above the snowy surface. Even there, you need to be careful. The tale is told of a photographer who leaned too far out of a window and did not see the bear below. However, the bear saw him and the end of the story was ugly. Also, during the polar bear season, people usually walked down the center of the street to avoid a possible bear near a corner. Another story is of the man who broke into a restaurant one night and stole a bunch of meat which he wrapped inside his coat. While getting away with his food, he mistakenly went on the sidewalk and turned a blind corner where a passing polar bear hungrily thanked him for dinner.

Polar bears walk more like cats than other bears and seem to glide over the frozen tundra. They do a lot of play fighting – sometimes standing on their hind feet and sparring like a pair of boxers. Like many visitors, our small video crew was accompanied by an armed guard carrying a 12-gauge shotgun filed with solid shot. On a couple of occasions, our guard felt it necessary to send a warning shot over a bear's head. We got some terrific footage which CNN used repeatedly over a period of several years. I still wish I could return for another polar bear trip but global warming has changed and reduced their habitat.

On another occasion, CNN embraced my idea to do a multi-day series of live reports from different parts of the Sierra and talk about climate issues. Using a satellite truck, we would start in heavily visited Yosemite National Park, work our way up to the Yosemite high country – Tuolumne Meadows – then down to Mono Lake, Mt. Whitney and the Owens Valley. For the first day, we were joined by another photographer friend – the renowned Galen Rowell –who took us to the sites of some of his famous shots. Park Service managers in Yosemite were very helpful with interviews and insight. But when we crossed out of the national park territory and onto Forest Service land the attitudes changed. We had repeatedly asked for a senior Forest Service person to join us for a live shot, only to be brushed off. So, during each live shot, I would close by saying that we were being stiffed by the Forest Service.

By the time we reached the Mt. Whitney area, the Forest Service caved in and their director flew out from Washington, D.C. to go on camera with us. The next day, we drove up to Horseshoe Meadow which provided a wonderful overview of the Owens Valley on the eastern side of the Sierra. People living as far away as San Diego complained of the salt laden dust storms that blew out of Owens Lake and polluted their air. We were able to shoot one of those storms so that our viewers could see it all. It was a perfect way to wrap up the series of reports. We then returned to Los Angeles where our material was edited into an hour long special.

It was also during the CNN days when the 1992 Rodney King riots erupted. Four white police officers accused of beating black motorist Rodney King were acquitted by a white jury. I was en route back to Los Angeles during a break in presidential campaign coverage and was told to immediately get to the Los Angeles CNN Bureau to join a waiting camera crew. I did and hopped into a white news van which was driven to the heart of the rioting. We had not been there long when a man came out of a looted liquor store waving a loaded revolver. He took one look at our news van and opened fire. Our driver froze, and I had to hit him to get him to step on the gas and get us out of there. Meanwhile, the obviously intoxicated man fired all six rounds in his gun at us. Fortunately, he was so drunk that all six rounds missed the van. We kept reporting throughout the night – often going on live from various locations – until things finally calmed down and we returned to the office. The area around our Hollywood office was deserted and eerily quiet. Never before had I seen that normally busy street so empty.

# CHAPTER 26

In the political field, George H.W. Bush was elected president after Reagan left the White House. I did not know him well and we had clashed occasionally both while he was in Congress and later as Vice President. I knew his Vice President – Dan Quayle—much better because Quayle was from Indiana and had served in the Senate. From time to time, Quayle would complain privately that it was hard to get the president to focus on domestic issues rather than international affairs. That focus may have played a role in the 1992 campaign when Bush sought re-election while running against Democrat Bill Clinton later in 1992. I became CNN's lead correspondent covering the Clinton campaign.

Tom Bradley was mayor of Los Angeles at the time and Dee Dee Myers was his press person. She was good at the job and, as the Clinton campaign got underway, I strongly urged the top strategists for Clinton to recruit Dee Dee. They did and she went on to become the first woman to serve as White House press secretary. Dee Dee later went to work for Warner Brothers in Los Angeles.

Clinton's campaign was fascinating, albeit exhausting, to cover. Like Lyndon Johnson, Clinton seemed to have an extra energy gland that could keep him going for hours on end. His campaign theme song was Fleetwood Mac's *Don't Stop Thinking About Tomorrow* and Clinton often campaigned as though there was no tomorrow. Nonetheless, he seldom was boring. He had a remarkable memory and sometimes we would try to trip him up with quotes from one book or another. More often than not he was able to identify the book.

Clinton also was seriously savvy about press coverage. At a campaign stop in New England, I was busy typing out the day's story when I felt the presence of someone behind me. It was Clinton reading the story over my shoulder and offering up a couple of fresh quotes. At another point, I had finished a truly terrible and dull interview with Clinton's running mate Al Gore. In desperation, I reached out to Dee Dee and said we could not use the Gore interview. Minutes later, she got back to me and said that Clinton would make a hole in his schedule so that he could do a fresh interview. The end result was classic Clinton and a lot better.

Clinton's campaign staff, itself, was an interesting collection of people run by the very smart James Carville who came up with the phrase "It's the Economy, Stupid." After leaving the White House, James went on to become a fixture on television news programs because of his ability to turn a phrase, as did fellow strategist Paul Begala who also was well liked by reporters for his way with a good quote.

Clinton was on the receiving end of a fair amount of teasing about his weight and physical fitness. Al Gore was seriously interested in staying in shape and went running most mornings. Some of us sometimes also went running. Clinton took up running too, especially when we all were staying in Little Rock. But WJC often seemed to find McDonalds irresistible. One vivid memory is of the campaign motorcade rolling down the highway in Arkansas when a McDonalds appeared ahead. All of us on the campaign bus started guessing that Clinton would have the motorcade turn around. And that is exactly what he did. Suddenly that McDonalds became the busiest eatery in the area as the entire Clinton campaign group descended upon it. Eventually, after leaving the White House, Clinton – spurred by a series of heart problems – became a vegan, lost considerable weight and appeared much healthier.

Election night in Little Rock was a full-on party time. The Clinton team was confident they would win and the crowd was very large. In his victory speech, Clinton declared that his goal was *"to bring our people together as never before so that our diversity can be a source of strength in a world that is ever smaller, where everyone counts and everyone is part of America's family."* The Clintons decided to vacation on Hilton Head Island in South Carolina. There was not a lot to report on most days but it was decided that I should do a round up report from there. Unfortunately, there was not much video with which to work. So, we decided to basically do a three-camera report with me on camera most of the time. Miraculously, we pulled it off.

In the interim, I was asked by the management folks at CNN if I wanted to return to Washington as White House correspondent. After giving it some thought, I said that I had done the White House on three separate occasions and preferred not to uproot my family in California for a repeat performance in Washington. A couple of days later, I was informed that a new White House correspondent had been selected and he had no television experience and not much political experience. His name was Wolf Blitzer from the Jerusalem Post. I was asked to show him around and bring him up to speed on the transition team and the key players. That was fine with me and I set to work arranging some meetings for Wolf with the Clinton team. Unfortunately, Wolf was not interested. In fact, he generally appeared disinterested, poorly informed and not the smartest reporter I ever had met. I called the CNN Bureau Chief in Washington to report on Wolf's progress and asked if they really were serious about making him the White House correspondent. I expressed my serious doubts. Then I was given the answer to it all. The bureau chief said that he understood that Wolf may not be all that bright but "his name is Wolf and viewers will like that." The rest, as we all know, is history.

Nonetheless, for the eight years of the Clinton Administration, I had reliable access to several people on the White House staff including press secretary Mike McCurry – one of the true good guys in Washington politics. When Bill Clinton was caught having an Oval Office affair with a young intern – Monica Lewinsky – I was stunned and dismayed by the efforts of the Clinton staff to manage the problem and suspected that the president himself was part of that problem. I called Mike and offered a suggestion – namely that the president address a gathering of ministers at their annual meeting and that he arrange to have the Rev. Jesse Jackson introduce him. Jackson, himself, had a reputation for womanizing and I thought his presence might get some of the sting off of Clinton. After some back and forth, the president agreed and so did Jackson who delivered strong words of support after Clinton spoke delivering his personal mea culpa. Although the Lewinsky affair did not entirely go away, things calmed down after that.

On another occasion, George and I boarded the ship The Searcher for a journey to Baja California and the Sea of Cortez to photograph the annual gathering of gray whales where the females give birth to their young. These females reach 50 feet in length and weigh up to 40 tons. They are proud of their babies and seem to like attention. Several mothers brought their infants up to the inflatable boat that we road in to just show them off. In one case, one of the baby whales became curious and put his eye right up against our underwater camera lens and stared back at us. On another visit, one of the female whales rose up beneath us and balanced our small boat on her back and took us for a ride.

**Baby Gray Whale playing.**

# CHAPTER 27

Back in Los Angeles, I began working on a story involving the American Red Cross. Partnering with producer Chuck Conder, we scoured through a stack of documents that had been leaked to us. They included legal action then underway against the people in Red Cross headquarters in Washington, D.C. The more we dug, the uglier things got. We uncovered evidence that the Red Cross had been sending HIV contaminated blood to American troops in Iraq. Then we found evidence that the Red Cross top executives had stashed funds in an offshore account in the Caribbean that they planned to use to cover the costs of any likely lawsuits. And on it went. Eventually, we became aware that my friend Connie Chung was working on a similar story for CBS. Chuck and I decided that we should put our story on the air promptly. Our bureau chief in Los Angeles called the story the best investigative work he ever had seen. The senior producers in Atlanta were less than thrilled, however, and insisted that we fly to Atlanta and review all of our material with the company's attorneys. We did so, and the attorneys' verdict was that we had an iron clad story and one of them declared he would love to defend it in a courtroom if the Red Cross sued. Nonetheless, the Atlanta producers were furious, saying that we were besmirching the good name of the Red Cross. And so, they did their best to bury the story. Then Connie's story ran on CBS and it was very similar to ours. When combined, the two stories – ours and Connie's – forced the top brass at the Red Cross to resign and Elizabeth Dole was named the new director. She credited Connie and I for a job well done.

However, the Atlanta producers – for reasons no one ever understood – made it clear that they were hunting for my head. Stories that I pitched went nowhere and I was told that I had too many story ideas when I should only be doing what I was told. Shortly thereafter, I was offered a job as Richard Riordan's media consultant in his campaign to become mayor of Los Angeles and I took it.

Riordan is/was an interesting man. A self-made millionaire, he was bidding to replace outgoing mayor Tom Bradley – a good and decent man who had served the people of Los Angeles very well. Riordan – a moderate Republican – was well positioned to win the election. He was a natural campaigner and people liked him. In a sense, he was a forerunner to Donald Trump. Riordan was by no means crude or thoughtless, but he was wealthy and sometimes thought he was a bit entitled. Also, he had the attention span of a gnat. Nonetheless, he asked me to help write his inauguration speech and he let me include a quote from Robert Kennedy in the speech. But it was clear that I would not be part of his official team at city hall which was fine with me and we parted on friendly terms. Later, he autographed his autobiography for me.

In the middle of all this, my son Dylan became seriously ill. He had been putting on an unusual amount of weight and it clearly was not normal. Medical tests showed that he was suffering from Cushing's Disease due to a very rare tumor on his pituitary gland. The outlook was grim – a life expectancy of only two more years at best. He was then just 8 years old. His mother Mariko Fukuda and I decided to take the risk of brain surgery and Dr. Martin Weiss put together a surgical team and – because this was so rare –an extra group of 10 doctors also was added to the surgery room – including a doctor from Russia. My friend Bob Rosenquist had interned with Dr. Weiss and Bob called him to say, "Marty…I will be looking over your shoulder." Another medical friend – Dr. Yuri Parisky – was in the surgery room observing. After what seemed forever, Yuri Pariski came out and told us the surgery had been successful! However, Dylan remained in the hospital for several weeks and then was transferred to Children's Hospital for what would be almost three years of return visits and check-ups.

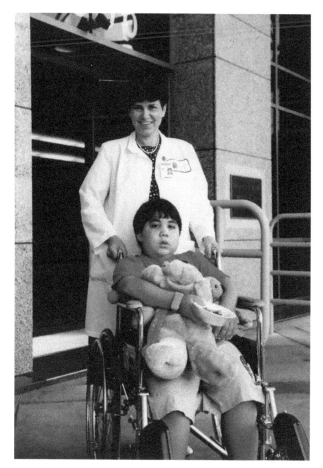

**Dylan Leaving the Hospital**

For some reason, both youngsters had caught the attention of President Clinton – probably encouraged by friends (and White House senior staffers) John Emerson and Dee Dee Meyers. So, periodically I would get a call from the White House instructing me to be sure that both Dylan and Courtney would be waiting in the secure area at LAX to greet the president when he arrived for a visit. And this brings me to a classic Bill Clinton story.

One day, Courtney informed me that she did not want to get excused from class to see President Clinton. "We get to see him a lot," she said. I informed her that standing up the President was not an option. However, when the president came off the plane, I told him how Courtney wanted to stay in school. Well, he walked past all the dignitaries, knelt down in front of her and informed Courtney that he was very impressed that she wanted to stay in class and not take time out. He carried on that way for about three minutes and, by the time he finished, I would swear that Courtney was floating a good foot off the ground. Clinton then borrowed a pen and some paper and personally wrote out an excuse for both Dylan and Courtney to take to their teachers at Ivanhoe Elementary.

Dylan went on to become a star high school football player at John Marshall High where, as captain, he led the team to the Los Angeles coliseum when they played for the conference title. Then on to UC Berkeley where he earned good grades and a 3$^{rd}$ degree black belt in judo which resulted in him becoming coach of the Berkeley Judo Team and working with an Olympic prospect.

**Dylan Graduating from Berkeley**

Courtney played basketball and ran track at John Marshall High School and graduated as class Valedictorian with one of the school's highest GPAs ever. Then she was off to UCLA and finally to law school at the University of Washington.

**Courtney Being Congratulated by City
Councilman Tom LaBonge**

Meanwhile, daughters Laura and Lynne raised families of their own in Utah and Oregon respectively.

# CHAPTER 28

For quite some time, I had thought about starting my own production and photography company. Over the years, I had worked with a number of truly talented people. Among them were ABC's long time West Coast producer Roger Scott, videographer Dave Carstens, video editor Jamie Tullo, camera operator and producer Scott Meyer to name just a few. They and others became the core of my new company – *Image* Associates. We produced and shot for Bombardier Aerospace and its SuperScooper firefighting aircraft that were introduced to Los Angeles and still are used to fight California wildfires. They are amazingly effective because of their quick response time and the large loads of water that they drop very accurately on a raging fire. During this time, I also met Gloria Cortes who became my wife and partner in the creation of *Image Associates*. We also produced and delivered videos for Lockheed, the U.S. Chamber of Commerce, the AARP, various political campaigns, California Attorney General and now U.S. Senator Kamala Harris, client support for Englander Associates and Cerrell Associates among others. We also did a special report on Harp Seals in the Magdalene Islands off the Canadian coast that always has stayed with me. Harp seals are endangered because poachers – mostly French Canadian fishermen – kill their adorable pups for their lovely white fur which was made into expensive hats and coats sold mostly in Europe. The snowy white pups often are clubbed to death. I was picked for this special because I spoke French which was essential. During conversations with the seal hunters, I came to understand how their fur trade was essential to their economy, but I still hated the practice. Visiting the area via helicopter, I was warned repeatedly to be careful where I stepped. A patch of thin ice could plunge an unwary person into water so frigid that survival was very difficult and probably unlikely. One of my all-time favorite photos is a close-up of a fearless baby harp seal with which I was almost eyeball to eyeball.

We produced a special on grey whales near the Santa Barbara Channel for the Outdoor Life Network, a special video for the good people at Yosemite National Park, a series of stories for the Los

Angeles Times and more. My wife Gloria Cortes and I also spent a lot of time as still photographers shooting scenic and wildlife photos throughout much of the western United States, including Hawaii and Alaska. The latter included a week shooting grizzly bears around the Cook Inlet.

Capturing images in the wilds of the western United States is both challenging and exciting. From time to time, we shot with famed photographer and friend George Lepp and with my pal Galen Rowell who died along with his wife Barbara in a small plane crash in the eastern Sierra.

I happen to like mountain lions. They may be my favorite predator. And, contrary to public opinion, they are not particularly dangerous unless you do something stupid to provoke them or if the big cat is ill or old. Typically, they also have a cat's curiosity.

One time, George Lepp and I were shooting on game ranch that provided animals for movie and television shoots. George stopped to change the film in his camera and a tiger leaped on him, knocking him to the ground. The tiger's handler started running and hit the big cat like a football linebacker slamming into a runner. The tiger flew through the air and landed on the ground with an expression that seemed to say, "what did I do?" George was not injured.

Gloria became fascinated shooting wildflowers everywhere we went, and she has become quite expert at doing so—often taking advantage of our living not far from the Antelope Valley where California poppies frequently bloom creating hillsides full of orange color.

At the same time, I became the host of two nationally syndicated television programs – *Beyond the Beltway* which included a rotating panel of smart people interviewing equally smart guests about the politics of the day and *A Conversation With...* in which I delivered one-on-one interviews with people from many walks of life who I thought the audience would find interesting. They included elected officials, presidential hopefuls, community activists and people from science and education. One of the most popular was space science engineer Gentry Lee who communicated such an enthusiasm for describing the potential of various programs that he was asked to return several times. These programs were underwritten by Century Cable which boasted television outlets all across the country in major population centers. Unfortunately, Century Cable eventually was bought by Time Warner, which drove the programming into a downward spiral as senior executives said to me they had no interest in public interest programming. Thus, after several successful years, our programs faded away due to lack of financial support. However, both of these programs did provide highly regarded public service and – as a believer in public service and information programming – I found their demise disappointing and Time Warner's approach clearly dominated by simple greed.

Not too long after this, some strange and violent behavior occurred in our neighborhood. A young actor – Johnny Lewis – had rented an apartment in the home of our next door neighbor. We found his behavior strange. Then one day he attacked and killed his landlady and our good friend Catherine Davis. I had known Cathy and her daughter Marnie for many years. Cathy was a nurturing soul who did her best to help both the famous and the not so famous who showed up at her door from time to time. She was a neighborhood legend and very well liked. After killing Cathy, Johnny Lewis attacked a man who was helping paint our house – causing the man to lose sight in one eye. When I tried to stop him, he swung an arm that sent me flying across our large deck. He appeared to be on some kind of drugs. I am a $3^{rd}$ degree black belt in Judo and boxed in high school. So, I know how to throw a punch and I hit Lewis in the temple with everything I had. He just looked at me as though I was a gnat and started trying to break into our house. I picked up a wooden bench and hit Lewis with it. The bench shattered but Lewis did not stop. However, he did pause for a moment and my wife went at him with her fingernails clawing his face. Then, I joined her and our injured painter trying to keep Lewis from getting through our door. With all our strength, the three of us slammed the heavy wooden door on his arm – once, twice, three times – until he cried out and then he spun around and literally leaped over the fence between our home and Cathy's. He climbed up on Cathy's roof and we lost sight of him, but he appeared to have fallen from the roof onto the driveway, shattering his head. I suspect we had done enough damage that he was unable to balance on the roof and took the fatal fall. Good riddance.

# CHAPTER 29

At this stage of my life, I have few regrets and much for which to be thankful. My wife Gloria is a genuine blessing and I am grateful for her company every day. My children – Laura, Lynne, Dylan and Courtney – listed in descending order by age are true delights. Together they nagged me into writing this memoir. We enjoy their company whenever we can get together with them. Getting together seems less frequent as they mature and have their own lives to live. Playing tennis and music has kept me relatively sane over the years. Along with me, my tennis racquets and guitars have aged rather gracefully – the graceful part applying to the racquets and instruments which has allowed me to continue to enjoy them. My favorite is a vintage Fender Telecaster that I purchased brand new in 1955 and have kept tightly in my grasp ever since. It is signed to me by guitar maker Leo Fender which his assistant informed me made it one of only six such guitars signed by Leo over the years. He reportedly refused to sign one for Rolling Stones guitarist Keith Richards. A few years later, guitarist Eric Clapton, one of my guitar heroes, wanted to buy it during an interview that I did with him, but I said absolutely not. Hopefully it will remain in the family and be cared for by Dylan whose own guitar playing is truly fine.

I owe special thanks to my backpacking and skiing and photography pal Dr. Bob Rosenquist, NBC network videographer Jim White about whom so many tales abound, NBC political producer Jim Connor whose insights always helped clarify my reporting, video editor par excellence Jamie Tullo – another NBC alum – who turned the rocks that I brought to her into gems. Bob Goldstein and Ollie who read all the pages and offered outstanding advice. Jules Witcover for his generous comments. My brother Tom who always has been available for discussion and insight on the phone. Finally, thank you to everyone who picked up this book and managed to wade through its many pages. I hope you enjoyed reading them as much as I did writing them.

Let me close with a quote from Robert Kennedy that seems appropriate to our times.

*In our wise and elaborate constitutional structure of checks and balances, the press is a check on government itself; giving content and meaning and force to that popular judgment and will which is the soul and design of democracy. Your obligation is not in your relationship to government but to the people, never confusing the nation with those who are its temporary leaders...We also know that the day you are unanimously joined in praise of officials and policies, when power is held in awe and skepticism disappears – on that day democracy will begin to wither.*

# INDEX

# ABOUT THE AUTHOR

Author *Zen & The Cross Country Skier, Wild & Wonderful-*
*Images of the American West & Of Presidents & Predators*

Dan Blackburn is a veteran broadcast and print journalist and photographer who has served as a national correspondent for major broadcast networks covering the White House, Congress and presidential campaigns as well as the space program and environmental issues. He had a close relationship with Robert Kennedy and covered Kennedy from the time he was elected to the Senate through to his presidential campaign and subsequent burial in Arlington National Cemetery. He also has been a contributing writer for the Washington Post, Los Angeles Times and other publications and his photographs have been widely printed.

Dan Blackburn also is the author of two previous books – the popular Zen & the Cross Country Skier and the photo book Wild & Wonderful featuring his photography of the western United States.

.

CPSIA information can be obtained
at www.ICGtesting.com
Printed in the USA
LVHW07s1046230718
584632LV00024B/738/P